THE PEOPLE OF GOD

by

Fr. Karl Pruter

WILDSIDE PRESS

www.wildsidebooks.com

TABLE OF CONTENTS

Chapter I
The People of God 1

AT THE PORTAL

Chapter II
How To Find a Faith 6

Chapter III
An Invitation 12

Chapter IV
Do I need God? 16

Chapter V
The Laborers in the Vineyard 20

Chapter VI
Don't Go Away Mad 25

Chapter VII
Doing Your God Chosen Thing 31

Chapter VIII
I'm Not Very Religious But— 34

Chapter IX
Victory Over the Cross 39

Chapter X
Through Him All Things Are Possible 43

Chapter XI
Thy Faith Has Made Thee Whole 46

Chapter XII
Why Have You Forsaken Me? 49

Chapter XIII
Be Ye Perfect 53

Chapter XIV
Peace of Mind 56

Chapter XV
Simon the Cyrenian 61

IN HIS HOUSE

Chapter XVI
The Fellowship of Christ 67

Chapter XVII
Pentecost 70

Chapter XVIII
Friends of Jesus 72

Chapter XIX
Praying for the People of God 75
Chapter XX
Walking in the Spirit 77
Chapter XXI
The Lord Has Need of Us 80

PITFALLS OF THE SPIRITUAL LIFE

Chapter XXII
Pitfalls of the Spiritual Life 85
Chapter XXIII
Be Thankful 88
Chapter XXIV
Faith in Turbulent Times 92
Chapter XXV
We Are Strangers in This World 98
Chapter XXVI
The Enigma of the Cross 103
Chapter XXVII
Counting the Cost 106
Chapter XXVIII
In Times of Spiritual Dryness 111
Chapter XXIX
Judge Not 117
Chapter XXX
St. Stephen 122
Chapter XXXI
The Martha Syndrome 125

AT HIS TABLE

Chapter XXXII
What Do You See 131
Chapter XXXIII
This Do for the Re-Presenting of Me 134
Chapter XXXIV
Celebration 137

BEFORE HIS THRONE

Chapter XXXV
To Do Good for the Lord's Sake 143

Chapter XXXVI
Who Are You? 145

Chapter XXXVII
Here Am I 147

Chapter XXXVIII
Filled With the Spirit 149

Chapter XXXIX
Today Be in Paradise With Him 152

Chapter XL
Enthusiasm 155

Chapter XLI
Rejoice 158

Chapter XLII
Praise Ye the Lord 161

I
THE PEOPLE OF GOD

In our chaotic, confused, and evil world, dare we label any as the people of God?

Too often throughout history people have claimed for themselves this proud distinction. In fact, it was often the least god-like that boasted that they were, indeed, God's people.

Yet it is clear that not all the world is ready to ignore God, deny God, or willingly defy God.

There does exist in the world a rather substantial number of people, perhaps yourself included, who want to serve Him.

What distinguishes them as "people of God" is their desire to serve Him. They are set apart from the rest of the world merely by their knowledge that they are in this world to give service to their Creator.

It is true that they all too often fail to give Him proper service. Yet, they too are aware of this, and their awareness of their shortcomings is another distinguishing mark that sets them apart. For we live in a world that not only does not serve God but is ignorant of the fact.

The people of God know that God has given us clear and definite directions for living. To them the Ten Commandments are living guides and cannot be ignored nor compromised.

When they fail to live up to them they not only feel guilty, but they know they ought to be feeling guilty.

If the rest of the world regards such feelings as unhealthy, the people of God know that the disease is the cause of the guilt and not the guilt per se.

They know that sin is a reality that must be dealt with and that sin cannot be explained away but only repented, and atoned for, in order to receive the forgiveness of a generous God.

The people of God also know that this world is not their home. They seek that heavenly Kingdom for which they were created. God did not create man in order that he might be forever estranged from God, but He created him that he might be reconciled with Him, and with Him, and through Him enjoy eternal life. He would have man come to Him and live with Him in His heavenly Kingdom.

In none of this do the people of God believe that they are better than others, for they believe all men are called to this life.

The only difference is that they believe. And believing that they are called to Him, they continually strive to find Him. Feeble though their efforts may be, they are on target. They know where they are headed, and each faltering step marks them as God's people.

Hence, these meditations are addressed not to those without faith, not to the unbelievers, but to all and to any who believe that God calls all men unto Him, and that they want to be citizens of the Kingdom of God.

At the Portal

II
HOW TO FIND A FAITH

We are told that we are saved by faith, but for many, finding a faith is a frustrating and bewildering experience.

In Somerset Maugham's book *The Razor's Edge* we have the story of Larry, who represents a modern pilgrim's search for faith. Poor Larry looks everywhere, but he does not once look in the manger at Bethlehem, or in a Church which bears the name of the One who was born there.

Of course, he didn't look there because Maugham and a whole host of modern intellectuals have convinced themselves that the Church no longer holds the key to spiritual knowledge. Yet, we must admit that had he looked in a church he might have heard some conflicting answers.

For example, had he entered a Protestant Church he would have been told that the answers he sought could only be found in Scriptures. What would have proved quite unsettling was the fact that no one could agree on what the Scriptures taught.

Had he gone on further and asked a Unitarian, he would be told that he didn't have to look any further than his own reason. Unfortunately, often men begin their spiritual odyssey only after their own reason has failed to provide them with satisfactory answers to life's basic questions. So it is no comfort to these men to be told to return to the false god which has already failed them.

The Lutheran would say that Christ has the answer, and so He does. The problem is that many a Lutheran, and Catholic too for that matter, is quite vague about how one goes about finding Christ.

The Methodist is apt to stress spiritual experience and feels no one really knows anything about the things of God until he has experienced them first hand.

Perhaps the most glib of all are Catholics, for often, without thinking about the doubts and needs of the questioner, they say the answers are to be found in the Church. One branch of the Church refines this to the point of saying that the Pope is infallible in matters of faith and morals. When people reject this over simplification of the Church's role they are not necessarily rejecting either the Church or the Pope. No pope has ever been loved and respected by more people than the late Pope John. One reason he was so loved was that he seemed so simple, so humble and so unlike any man who would claim to be infallible in anything but his desire to serve His God and people entrusted to his care.

The sorry thing is that each and all of these answers are right. Faith is to be found in Christ.

How could we who are Christians think otherwise? Since we teach that He lives and that He is present at every Mass, are we so foolish as to believe He cannot lead and guide us even as He led the twelve so many years ago?

How can we overlook the fact that the Bible holds more knowledge about man's search for God than any other book? Where else can man turn and learn so much about God? The differences in interpretation beg the issue, for in most we agree, and our disagreements are only a testimony to our blindness and do not affect the validity of the truth that is there.

Nor can we reject reason since it is God given and Christ Himself appealed to men on the basis of reason. He denounced us when we were blindly following the faith of our fathers and demanded that we examine, and as a result breathe life into the dead bones of, our inherited faith.

And what Christian dares substitute mere belief for religious experience? Until you have experienced the power of prayer you cannot talk intelligently about the subject. Until you have experienced the presence of Christ at the Mass, how can you subscribe to the doctrine of transubstantiation? Do you really believe Christ is present? If you say it a thousand times in your catechism lesson, but have never once experienced His presence, you do not believe it in the sense that a belief is an absolute certainty that something is true.

The real presence is not something arrived at in the mind, but experienced by the believer with all his being.

Since the Catholic answer is apt to be that spiritual truth is to be found in the Church, let us examine this premise last.

What precisely does this mean? Well, first of all it would be folly to overlook the Church's 2,000 years of experience. Surely she has learned much in this time and has much to say through the creeds and through the lives of her saints who have walked with God in a very close and personal way. But the Church does not say the truth is found only here.

It is as if you were with other people in a room that had many windows, and a play was taking place outside. If you look out of one window, I another, a third man another, a fourth man still another, and a fifth out of one, perhaps twelve feet away from the first, we would see different things, and everything from a slightly different angle. It would not be surprising if we were to quarrel about what we saw. Notice, if you will, the next time people discuss religion. Sooner or later the discussion will bog down because the different participants will seek final answers where they feel the final authority is to be found. The Protestant, with his authoritarian Bible, is apt to meet head on a Catholic with an authoritarian Church.

But why this exclusiveness? Can't we look out of all five windows? Dare we really close any one of them? I am sure that God means for us to use every means at our disposal to find him. The Church has learned that men must be taught, she has learned that men should study the Scriptures, it is the Church that tries to bring men into a first hand experience with Jesus, it is the Church that seeks to open men's minds, and no pastor is worthy to be called a shepherd who would be content to have any of his flock settle for a vicarious faith. Unless we experience these truths they are never ours.

To be truly Catholic means avoid the narrowness that must inevitably come when we stress only one means of finding truth. I believe that the Scriptures will lead me to truth, and I believe that reason also will lead me to truth. There is no contradiction here, for both have been given to me by God. Nor can there be a contradiction in what I learn. If I read something which is contrary to reason, it can only be because I do not know how to read or I do not know how to reason.

I taught reading a few years ago to some of Chicago's functional illiterates. That city alone has 40,000. We just assume that we all know how to read, even as we blindly assume we all know how to think logically. I have studied both reason and logic for half a lifetime, and, of course, have less assurance that I can do either of them well than the man who has studied neither of them.

It is for this reason, as much as any other that I must avail myself of every window to the truth. For only when all agree, can I say with any degree of certainty that "This I believe."

I cannot say "I believe in Jesus Christ" except that I know that the Church teaches that He lives, that the Scriptures verify this, that I have experienced His presence, and as an intelligent being, I can comprehend the meaning of what I have seen and experienced. When all these paths to truth lead to the same conclusions, I can with certainty, confidence, and trust proclaim my faith, knowing that I have at least not shut out the broad perspective for some narrow sectarian view.

For our God is too big to be seen through one narrow window of our soul. If your God is not big enough to help you meet your problems, perhaps you have limited your search to too few places. Like Larry in Maugham's book, you may have neglected the Church, or perhaps the Bible, your reason, your experience, or even Christ Himself.

God has provided so many instruments for you to find Him, and He does not hide Himself from us. So as this next Christmas approaches, will you resolve to open the windows that are closed and look out to Bethlehem and beyond, that the light that has come into the world may come into your heart and mind and dispel the darkness.

III

AN INVITATION

SECOND SUNDAY AFTER PENTECOST

GOSPEL: LUKE 14:16-24

> Then said he unto him, A certain man made a great supper, and bade many; And sent his servant at supper time to say to them that were bidden, Come: for all things are now ready. And they all with one consent began to make excuse. The first said unto him, I have bought a piece of ground, and I must needs go and see it: I pray thee have me excused. And another said, I have bought five yoke of oxen, and I go to prove them; I pray thee have me excused. And another said, I have married a wife, and therefore I cannot come. So that servant came, and shewed his lord these things. Then the master of the house being angry said to his servant, Go out quickly into the streets and lanes of the city, and bring in hither the poor, and the maimed, and the halt, and the blind. And the servant said, Lord, it is done as thou has commanded, and yet there is room. And the lord said unto the servant, Go out into the highways and hedges, and compel them to come in, that my house may be filled. For I say unto you, That none of those men which were bidden shall taste of my supper.

No lesson is more relevant to our time than today's gospel lesson. Jesus tells about many types of people who have received a wonderful invitation. Each is anxious to accept: but each has a reason, which he thinks is over-riding, that causes him to refuse.

What we have to keep in mind is that none is rejecting the invitation per se. It's that accepting the invitation demands a price. For one it means leaving his farm, which he feels needs attention that day, for another it's a new wife, and for a third its an investment in cattle. Each has something which he has given priority to; and although the invitation is intriguing, its lure is not strong enough, and the invited will not accept at the price he is going to have to pay. If only we could hear the gospel when we had nothing else to do! But God comes to us in the midst of life: he comes when we are busy with so many things. Sometimes our excuses are so lame—like "I work all week long and Sunday morning I like to stay in bed."

Sometimes they are critical. Like the man in Scripture who had a harvest to get in, we are often crises oriented. Our business, or our job, requires everything we have, lest everything go under.

A pastor who spends a life time in one place often sees a dreary procession of life passing through his study. A young man comes to him and pleads that he cannot take a serious interest in the church—now—because he is young and there is so much he wants to do and so much he wants to learn that he just doesn't have time to think about one more thing or to give himself in service. He next sees his pastor when he wants to be married, and often for a long time afterwards the church sees little of him, for he is attentive to his new wife.

When the children come he then pleads he must work so hard that Sunday is his only day of leisure and surely the pastor should understand.

As the years move on the excuses grow more varied, but they proceed with predictable regularity. Each time the invitation comes, as God touches the life on the Sacramental occasions, marriage, birth, baptism, the death of a parent, the times of crisis in sickness and trouble; it is considered, but put aside because the price seems too high.

No wonder so many today are looking for shortcuts. If God could only be found through drugs or through some new eastern cult. A few, by cutting the hard discipline out of Zen and embracing it in a denuded form, feel they have found a quick and easy way to enlightenment.

But Jesus has made it plain that there is no short road, no easy way, and that the approach to God demands much of us.

If anything, the price goes up with each passing year. For while others toil joyfully in God's vineyard, the undecided stand idly by, wondering if they will be allowed into the vineyard. The excuses have the effect of hardening our resistance, and soon we become satisfied with the humdrum, the dull, and the repetitious routine of daily life. In fashioning the world, God has almost done too good a job. No slum, no ghetto, and no prison, seems evil enough to make men want to escape by entering God's Kingdom.

We must, as Jesus told us, see the Kingdom of God as a pearl without price. Once we realize that God's offer of himself is so great, we shall gladly pay the price of acceptance. Sell all that you have in order to buy it, says Jesus.

But do we have so much? Is it really so difficult? Or have we closed our ears and eyes and hardened our hearts? Are we like difficult children, unwilling to come when we are called, but anxious to establish the fact that we shall answer in our own good time? If so, Jesus says it is our peril, "For the Lord of the feast said of those whom he had invited, "that none of those who were invited shall taste of my supper."

There is a demanding note in God's invitation. It is simply that the table is set, that all is in readiness, and that Christ would have us leave whatever we are doing and come unto Him!

IV

DO I NEED GOD?

PSALM 130:1-2

Out of the depths have I cried unto thee, O Lord, Lord, hear my voice: let thine ears be attentive to the voice of my supplications.

Whenever a priest meets new people, he discovers that the world seems to be about equally divided between those who wish to tell him that they know that they need God and those who wish to tell him that they are sure they don't need God.

Usually those who are most vociferous about NOT needing God very obviously need something or someone.

But what about the question, "Do I need God?" How shall we answer it?

To most of us, the most important factor in life is happiness. Those who contend that they don't need God often mean that they are quite happy without Him and, indeed, it is very possible to be happy without God. In fact, in some ways, many people would be happier without Him than with Him. For without God, we often are not troubled by conscience over the treatment we mete out to other people. We can be as selfish as we like and our sleep and happiness may be undisturbed. For

God does disturb the peace of the transgressor and one cannot be happy with God and live in sin. One must either forego sin or God and often we find it easier to forego God.

One must truly enjoy good to find happiness in the presence of God. But to the man for whom good is a pleasure, God is a welcome friend and companion who brings much joy.

But what about those whose life goal is wealth? Do they need God? Some of the great merchants and industrialists of the past have very emphatically answered, "No." They employed methods and ethics which God would have condemned, and so they waited until they had gathered their fortunes before beginning their life of good works.

As people observe those who climb to the pinnacle of economic success, they often rationalize their own failures and say that except for their own high moral and ethical standards they too might be rich. In short, those who aspire to wealth often feel not only that they do not need God, but that He would, indeed, be a handicap to their aspirations.

On the other hand, history provides many examples where the poor and downtrodden have become imbued with religion and in the course of two or three generations have risen high on the economic ladder. It does seem without question that most deeply religious people do not suffer from want. Of course, this is not the same as wealth, and it would be absurd to say that God exists for the purpose of making one wealthy.

Likewise it is certain He does not exist to insure your success by the standards of this world.

In fact, while many successful tycoons hasten to assure the world that they owe much of their success to their faith in God, the world views their claims with justified skepticism. In truth God says, "My ways are not your ways," and Jesus reminded his disciples time and time again that His Kingdom was not of this world.

In the 14th Century, a group of Christians appeared who put this whole question into new focus. They asked not, "Do we need God?" but they affirmed that God needs us. Man they argued was created because God was lonely. Hence they would be friends of God.

They looked at the world of God's creation and became convinced that God needed them.

Does God really need me? I believe he does. He needs me that He might have fellowship with other beings. Poor and imperfect as I am, God loves me and wants to converse with me. For there is but one God and without our fellowship, God would be alone in the universe of His own creation.

Secondly, God needs me because I am His creation. The creator is not complete without the objects of His creation. What His hand has shaped with His love belongs to Him, and without it, life for God would not be complete.

And, now consider for one moment. If the Almighty God needs me in order that He might find fulfillment, then how much more do I need Him that I might find fulfillment.

To find and have fellowship with my Creator must be the purpose for which I was made. How could I contend life was complete or that the purpose of my creation was fulfilled unless I find God?

For all the things that do not really matter—happiness, wealth, or success—I do not need God. But for the central things of life, I most certainly do. The life that does not long for God, that is not lonely for Him, is a life that is superficially lived and at the end of three score years and ten will pass away and the world will know it no more.

But to seek God, to find Him, and to have one's life and being with Him, is to fulfill the purpose of one's creation and to have life abundant and life eternal.

For those who know the true meaning of God's creation will cry out of the depths that God may be attentive to the voice of their supplications.

Like David they cry out of their need,

"My soul waits in silence for God alone." (Psalm 62:1)

V

THE LABORERS IN THE VINEYARD

GOSPEL: MATTHEW 20:1-16

For the kingdom of heaven is like unto a man that is an householder, which went out early in the morning to hire labourers into his vineyard. And when he had agreed with the labourers for a penny a day, he sent them into his vineyard. And he went out about the third hour, and saw others standing idle in the marketplace, and said unto them; Go ye also into the vineyard, and whatsoever is right I will give you. And they went their way.

Again he went out about the sixth and ninth hour, and did likewise. And about the eleventh hour he went out, and found others standing idle, and saith unto them, "Why stand ye here all the day idle? They say unto him, Because no man hath hired us. He saith unto them, Go ye also into the vineyard; and whatsoever is right, that shall ye receive.

So when even was come, the lord of the vineyard saith unto his steward, Call the labourers, and give them their hire, beginning from the last unto the first. And when they came that were hired about the eleventh hour, they received every man a penny. But when the first came, they supposed that they should have received more; and they likewise received every man a penny. And when they had received it, they murmured against the good man of the house.

Saying, These last have wrought but one hour, and thou hast made them equal unto us, which have borne the burden and heat of the day. But he answered one of them, and said, Friend, I do thee no wrong: didst not thou agree with me for a penny? Take that thine is, and go thy way: I will give unto this last, even as unto thee. Is it not lawful for me to do what I will with mine own? Is thine eye evil, because I am good? So the last shall be first and the first last: for many be called, but few chosen.

The owner of the vineyard would certainly be in trouble with any American labor union. At first glance what he has done seems like an out--rage to anyone's sense of justice.

The only justification he gives for his behavior is to point out that he did what he had agreed to. The first laborers had agreed upon what they considered a fair wage, and at the end of the day they received what was their due. The Lord of the vineyard felt he ought not to be criticized if he chose to be generous with those who came later. After all, it was his money and he could do with it as he chose. Why, he said, should anyone begrudge his generosity.

Most of us, upon reading the story, are inclined to agree, and still we feel unsatisfied. Something gnaws at us, and while it logically seems that everyone was treated correctly, emotionally we cannot accept the situation.

Our problem is that we are too earthbound to appreciate this analogy. If we would only keep in mind the nature of the vineyard. This is God's vineyard, and it is a great privilege and pleasure to work in it. Those who are allowed in are the fortunate ones, and those who must stand idle in the middle of the town are to be pitied. They have been kept out for most of the day. While the others were engaged in productive labor and worked side by side with the Lord, they had to endure the uncertainty, the purposelessness, and the aloneness of standing idle.

For is it not a pleasure to work for one's Lord? Is it not a pleasure to be productive with one's hands? Is it not a pleasure to have the assurance of one's place in God's scheme of things?

Those for whom labor is not a pleasure, or for whom God's order is a burden, can never appreciate this parable. They are like those who do not sin in this world, hoping to be compensated in the next. But our compensation is the righteous life, and our reward is not the penny but the labor in the vineyard. For those for whom the penny is payment have their reward and rail against those who seem to have an equal share of the material things of this life. They are like those who somehow feel God has been unjust to allow the wicked to enjoy the riches of this life, while the righteous struggle to make ends meet.

But what Christ is saying here is that when we come to God's heavenly vineyard He will treat all men equally. Those who come early will receive their reward. In a sense, they will receive more, for they will be able to leave behind the monotony and frustration of standing idle in the market place and take their rightful position in the Lord's vineyard. Those who are called later will not be forced to take less. Although they have had to stand outside, they are now received into the vineyard, even as those who are called earlier.

God seeks us all and beckons us to Him. There is nothing in the market place that should deter us or cause us to hesitate. But if we do, Christ is telling us here, it is never too late. God does have a place for us, and our only penalty shall be our self imposed idleness.

God is equally generous with those who find Him with relative ease and with those who find Him only after much suffering and hardship.

Some escape the labor and travail of the work early, but to others, the way to the Lord's vineyard is laid with pain, frustration and sorrow. They find God but only with difficulty. The very hardness of life breeds doubt and despair, and when at last they enter in, they fear that they will not receive the same treatment as those laborers who have come early and labored all day.

But the Lord of the vineyard is generous and rewards each man as he chooses.

Each man needs to concern himself with his own situation. If any should envy, it would be those who came late. For they have missed the labor in the cool of the morning; they have missed the pleasure of the Lord's presence. But these do not grumble, probably because they are grateful to be there at all.

For the Lord of the harvest will do with His own as He pleases, and to each man He will reward as he wills. But to us is given the assurance that there is always room for us in the Lord's vineyard, and we are beckoned to lay our burdens aside and partake of the Heavenly Kingdom.

VI

DON'T GO AWAY MAD!

As a child I can recall hearing this retort used on frequent occasions. I still can't quite tell you what it is supposed to mean, but I can tell when it was used, and I can tell you that the user was almost always insincere.

You see he wanted the person towards whom he directed the remark to do just the opposite, that is, go away **mad,** and above all to go **away.**

Of course this is what happens, because it usually takes place when there has been a disagreement over rules.

Johnny wants to play baseball but he doesn't like the rules. After a quarrel he walks off the field, and someone taunts him with the remark, "Don't go away mad!"

He may leave the area entirely or he may hang around. If he hangs around he pretends to be disinterested in the game, and he watches a beetle or an ant. He may even talk with other spectators and attempt to convince them that this game isn't worth watching, because he once saw a big league game where the people knew the rules.

The Bible is filled with people, grown people, who have gone away mad.

For example, there was the rich young man who wanted to know how to get eternal life. Jesus told him that he should sell what he had and give it to the poor. Jesus didn't advocate this for everyone, but he apparently knew this young man quite well. He surmised quite rightly that his man was too attached to his possessions to give them up even for eternal life.

The young man either didn't know that God demanded a loyalty that would admit no rival or he hoped Jesus would overlook it.

When Jesus reminded him that one had to choose literally between a love of God and the love of possessions, the young man "went away mad." If this was the rule, he didn't want to play.

And then there was Nicodemus who came to Jesus by night. He asked the same question and got a different answer. His money apparently was no problem, but his way of life was. Jesus told him he had to be born again. He had to become an entirely new person.

Poor old Nicodemus! He pretended he didn't understand what Jesus meant. But Jesus wouldn't let that go by and told Nicodemus he knew perfectly what He meant. He reminded him that he was a teacher of the Pharisees, and consequently he knew a great deal about the laws of God.

And when Nicodemus was reminded that he knew the rules, he went away mad. If we can believe tradition, he didn't stay mad, and came back to play the game according to the rules. But not many do that; today literally thousands desert the Church annually because they don't like the rules.

Sometimes the rules can seem quite tough and even heartless. For example, one young man came to Jesus with the ironclad excuse. At least he thought it was ironclad. Yes, he would follow Jesus; yes, he had no qualms about the rules; but first, he had to bury his father. One wonders if there were other occasions when he expressed the same keen interest in being a follower but had some other excuse. At any rate, Jesus said it wasn't good enough. "Let the dead bury their dead," he said.

Do you want to follow God? Then the rule says you must do it today, this instant. You want to think about it? What's to think about?

When you begin to think about this one, you find an excuse. It may be trivial, or it may be of great importance. The young man thought he had one of unquestioned importance, and when Jesus didn't accept it, he, like countless others before him, went away mad.

God is still confronted with those who can't accept the rules of life because of divided loyalty, their unwillingness to change or their prior commitments. The world is filled with those who have gone away mad. By hook or crook they would change the rules, if they could.

The advocates of the new morality aren't about to be born again. They have gone away mad.

They are standing on the side lines and arguing with any spectator who will listen that those that are playing the game according to God's laws don't really understand the rules.

They are not like the dissenters of a generation ago. In my generation, those that didn't like the rules were willing to argue that the referees were calling things foul that weren't. They felt pretty good if they could convince a lot of people that sin really wasn't sin, but was only labeled so because some people were old-fashioned and outdated. The advocates aren't content with that. Situational ethics enables them to go one step further. They not only don't want their fouls called, but they want some of their fouls to be labeled as hits. Whereas some of my generation tried to rationalize that one should not feel guilty about breaking the rules, today we have some of the same type saying you should feel good, because, after all, done in love, all things can be right.

I still would like to know what situation makes killing a good act? I still would like to know what situation makes fornication a good act? Or adultery or stealing, or slander? Changing the names isn't the solution. Going away mad never got anyone anything.

Oh, I am sure by now that some of you have concluded **I** missed the point that the advocates of the new morality are trying to make. What they are saying is that the rigid attitude towards the

Ten Commandments never was God's law, and Christ would, if He were alive today, support the same view.

So they stand in the sidelines trying to persuade those that are eager to believe them and those that are not, that the game should be played according to the rules of the new morality.

I am not about to buy it, and I suggest that you hesitate before you buy it.

Do you remember what happened the last time you heard the expression, "Don't go away mad?" The fellow that left the game, do you remember clearly what he was like? He argues about the rules. Said you were all wrong. But he didn't really get anyone very upset, because you and he both were aware that he damn well knew what the rules were. He wasn't really challenging the validity of the rules. He was going away mad because if the rules were going to work to his disadvantage, if they were going to be applied to him, he wasn't going to play. And that was all there was to it.

The fact that theologians and philosophers are cloaking their arguments in fine terms shouldn't deceive anyone.

The world has played by the Ten Commandments much too long to have any sore heads come along and threaten to quit the game.

If there is reason for change I am willing to listen, but so far I haven't heard any. If anything, we have played the game with too little attention to the rules. Maybe change is in order, but why in the direction of tearing down the rules?

It could go both ways—but before anything at all is done, I always feel it is wise to consult the inventor of the game, the referee; and unless my childhood recollections have failed, I always paid a lot of attention to the owner of the bat and the ball.

I still feel that way, and as long as it is God's game and his equipment that enables me to play the game of life, I'll listen to Him rather than to those I feel have gone away mad.

If you are having difficulty in deciding how you shall live, I have only this counsel.

If the Christian life presents any sort of challenge, think—if you can accept it without divided loyalties, prior commitments, or a love for the life you now live—

then live it!
if you can't
forget it!
but
"Don't go away mad!"

VII

DOING YOUR GOD-CHOSEN THING

GOSPEL: MATTHEW 21:19

And when he saw a fig tree in the way, he came to it, and found nothing thereon, but leaves only, and said unto it, Let no fruit grow on thee henceforward for ever. And presently the fig tree withered away.

In the story of the fig tree, Jesus dramatically tells us that God expects something from us.

One of the many books I enjoy is C. S. Lewis' *The Great Divorce*. It is a science fiction story of a busload of people who go to heaven, although many of them are obviously not ready for the life they will lead there.

One gentleman arrives protesting that he always did his best. He wasn't a saint, he said, and he had his faults, but nonetheless, he did his best by everyone. The angel in charge tries to point out two flaws in his argument. The first is the obvious one, that he couldn't honestly say that he did his best. Or to put it another way, his best was none too good. But even more important, why do so many think that as long as they have done right by their fellow man they have served God?

For the commandment of Jesus is, that first we love God, and then we do unto others.

Throughout the gospel of Jesus is the insistence that God must be served.

Now, it is true that He often turns our attention and our service toward others, but the direction must come from Him. Unless you are doing His will you are not serving Him. We are like children who shower our parents with gifts when all they want is our love. Or like parents who have given their children everything, but the gift of themselves.

Real service implies knowing the will of the one served. Unless we do this we often miss the real heart of the gospel.

During World War II, before this country was drawn into the conflict, I remember seeing a newspaper photo of a peace rally. Here a large group of people gathered to oppose those who would draw America into war. One glance at the picture was enough to convince me that we would be drawn into war. For the faces of these advocates of peace did not show love, but hatred. In short, in spirit, they were no different from those who openly called for war.

If peace is ever to come it can only come after we meet two conditions. First, we must be at peace with ourselves. Through love and love alone can peace be spread.

Secondly, our efforts must be God directed. Unless He directs our hearts, we shall easily become provoked by the opposition and substitute our efforts for divine healing.

The lesson of the fig tree not only demands that we serve, but very pointedly, whom we shall serve. God will not permit us to substitute service to others for service to Him. Nor will He allow each man to select his own kind of alternate service. We have an expression these days that I like. We say, "Each man should be doing his thing". I would just amend it to "each man should be doing his God-chosen thing." For God does have something for you to do.

For one it may be service in the building of His Kingdom. For another, it may be witness to those about. For another it may be the use of some special talent that will make someone's life richer.

For another, it may be the use of skills that will make the world a better place.

And in some measure, we are all called to serve, to witness, to use our skills to help our fellowman. The important thing is that all our efforts be directed by Him and to His glory.

Let each man do his GOD-CHOSEN THING!

VIII

I'M NOT VERY RELIGIOUS BUT...

GOSPEL: 18:14

I tell you, this man went down to his house justified rather than the other: for every one that exalteth himself shall be abased; and he that humbleth himself shall be **exalted**.

The story that Jesus tells is a simple one, and one that in our time takes a very peculiar twist. In Jesus' day the way to exalt yourself was to appear to be more religious than you were. Please note that the sin was not in appearing religious but in attempting to exalt oneself.

Men were as prone to seek status 2,000 years ago as they are today. Nothing has changed except the way in which one seeks it. Whereas in Jesus' day, among the Jews one received status by being or even seeming religious, today it is often the opposite.

While there are still some circles where religious faith confers status in the 20th Century, men as often as not find deep piety a stigma instead of a mark of distinction. Note how often you hear the phrase, even from staunch Christian people, "I am not very religious, but..." Too often when people take a stand they feel it necessary to disavow their own deep religious feelings.

In this week's issue of Time, the comment is made that "New male arrivals to Los Angeles have been known to hide the fact that they go to church, until they find they can safely be both unconventional and accepted. The word "unconventional" here refers to their non-status and peculiar habit of church attendance.

Here we meet Jesus' pharisee again, but in a strange new garb. The fact of the matter is that in our time more men and women seek to be exalted by appearing to be less religious than they really are.

Sometime make an experiment. When you hear someone whom you regard as religious speak disapprovingly of some type of conduct, ask him in an accusing tone, "I suppose you oppose this because you are religious." I guarantee you he will deny that he is religious, and he will deny that his religion has anything to do with his feelings on the issue. He will then proceed to give you what he believes are more acceptable reasons for his attitude towards the question.

Occasionally you get the refreshing statement, "I feel the way I do because I am a religious person." Why not, if it is true?

In most cases it certainly won't give you an exalted position, and in any event you haven't made a claim to living well or badly, merely that you are religiously inclined and that, in this particular instance, it affects your attitude or behavior. After all, you know, it should!

Living as we do in a world that is only partially Christian, we often find it hard to know when our faith is a mark of distinction, and when it invites persecution.

A good illustration of this is the word puritan and puritanical. once these words were held in high esteem and today nobody wants to be labeled a puritan or have it said that his outlook was puritanical.

So hypocritical and pharisaical have we become that we have been silenced in many areas of art and morality.

Some of us tend to deplore what has happened to the good old American family motion picture. But if a picture is produced of which we don't approve, all someone has to do is say, "Don't be a puritan," and our protest is silenced. What's wrong with being a puritan? Or do you think that God is not?

The flood of books, plays, movies and periodicals of questionable taste can only be stemmed when enough people are willing to say, "That isn't for me, because it's contrary to my religion." Instead we are afraid to put it in those terms and try to ignore what is happening to our society and ourselves. Obviously, among the millions who attend salacious movies, read *Playboy* Magazine and the tons of pornographic and near pornographic books, there must be many members of churches and synagogues. What is the reason for it, and does our text tell us anything about it?

I'm convinced that most of these people are deathly afraid that their neighbors will consider them narrow-minded if they apply their faith to the arts and literature.

If you want status in our society, you must not appear to be religious, especially if it is going to have an effect upon your artistic likes and dislikes. If you prefer "Ave Maria" to Rock and Roll, it is all right if the preference is solely on the merits of the music and if you are willing to admit that both are equally good but you just happen to prefer the one over the other. But, lest the neighbors think that your attendance at Mass every Sunday and your preference for classical and religious music is making a prude or a fanatic out of you, having *Playboy* around the house will prove how broad-minded you are.

Hypocrisy has indeed gone the full turn of the wheel.

Parents who are contributing substantially to build churches, that their children might learn what is good and right, must prove to themselves and their neighbors that God doesn't affect all their thoughts and actions by attending the latest dirty movie, "Who's Afraid of Virginia Wolf?" In so doing they are contributing hard cash to an industry that will see that they get more movies of this type, and thereby make the task of training their children ever harder.

What are we trying so hard to prove? Not that we aren't religious, because many of us are. We are trying to do what the Pharisee was trying to do, receive public acceptance. But all through the Christian gospel is the admonition to seek only the approval of God. For truly religious people this is indeed a blessing, for it enables them to be themselves.

It is not faith that tries to make people be something they are not. All too often it is the irreligious, the unchurched people, and the atheistic that would remold and reshape people.

Many of us are just naturally inclined to acknowledge the presence and the glory of God. We feel thankful for our life and our daily bread, and we would give Him thanks. We love the things of God and we would live the life He expects of us.

We love good and hate evil, and this is our natural behaviour. We are religious, and there is no good reason why we should appear otherwise. In admitting to this we are often forced to humble ourselves before our neighbors. But Christ tells us that we need not fear, for in so doing, in due time, we shall be exalted.

IX

VICTORY OVER THE CROSS

EPISTLE: I Corinthians 1:20

Where is the wise? where is the scribe? where is the disputer of this world? hath not God made foolish the wisdom of this world?

As an Old Catholic, I suspect that any faith which calls itself "old" leaves itself wide open to ridicule. For our world is suspicious of anything that is not the latest and the newest. We have new math, new morality and even a modernized Roman Catholic Church.

More and more people are being tempted to change, to modify, and even drop those dogmas of the past which they find not to their liking.

The doctrine of Christ crucified has suffered suprisingly little from direct attack. For the most part, the modern church has tended to ignore it, and like men of Paul's day, find it a stumbling block and foolishness. The doctrine demands too much of us and calls for sacrifices many of us are not prepared to make.

When the great Napoleon was ruler of France he found the doctrines of the church an enigma and felt in her attachment to God's heavenly kingdom a threat to the creation of Napoleon's own more earthly kingdom. He asked one of his aides whether they couldn't create a new religion to replace the Catholic Church. The reply was "Most certainly, all they would have to do was to kill someone and have him rise again on the third day." Napoleon had to be reminded of the fact of the cross.

This is central to the church's teaching. Without the cross the religion that won the hearts and loyalty of the French would not exist. Like Napoleon, many of the church people may have found the cross a burden. But unlike Napoleon they realized its necessity.

For first of all, it represents a price that must be paid for sin. What man does not have some sin that must be atoned for? To think that we can live and not pay the cost of our errors is to fly in the face of reality.

Man's hate, greed, and selfishness inevitably produces war, which maims and kills indiscriminately. Willingly or unwillingly, millions pay the cost of war.

John Doane said, "No man is an island." When the drunkard gets into his car, regarding his drinking as a private vice, who knows what innocent child will help bear the burden of that man's sin. The slaughter on our highways is but one of the ways that we share the cost of one another's carelessness, and sin. This is a fact of life that even Napoleon could not escape.

But the cross is more than a place of atonement, it is also a place of reconciliation. Here God and man meet. Because Christ was also truly man, there had to be a cross. For as man, Christ had to bear the burden of sin.

As God, Christ could forgive the thief on the cross.

Each hanging there knew the cost of sin, and they knew of its expensive atonement. In paying the cost, they could face the judge of heaven and earth and dare to ask for a heavenly kingdom. Under no other circumstances can one face God and ask for so great a gift.

And the miracle of the cross is that the request was granted to both. Christ spoke to the thief and promised that that very day he would be with Him in paradise.

Easter destroyed once and for all the myth that life was limited to this world. For Christ's victory over the cross gives life a new perspective.

The man who tramples his fellowman into the dust in order to advance himself in business or industry believes his few years here constitute all there is to life. Consequently if he doesn't get it now, what else is there?

But the Christian builds for eternity. He seeks to mold himself after the pattern of Christ, that he might be fit to dwell forever in the presence of God. Perhaps the Christian is kinder only because He knows He has time to be kind. The Christian is not pushed or squeezed and compressed into the traditional three score years and ten. The treasures he seeks and saves are such that moths and rust can not consume.

A Napoleon is driven to plunder the world, because the world of Napoleon is so small. The only treasures he knows are here and other men possess them.

The Christian seeks not what other men possess but what they do not possess. In fact, he seeks what they have rejected and willingly picks up the rejected cross and follows Christ to Golgotha. There he meets not death, but a reconciliation with God the Father, and the fulfillment of Christ's promise that he would have life abundant and life eternal.

X

THROUGH HIM ALL THINGS ARE POSSIBLE

GOSPEL: MATTHEW: 13:24-30

Another parable put he forth unto them, saying, The Kingdom of Heaven is likened unto a man which sowed good seed in his field: but while the man slept, his enemy came and sowed tares among the wheat, and went his way. But when the blade was sprung up, and brought forth fruit, then appeared the tares also. So the servants of the householder came and said unto him, Sir, didst not thou sow good seed in thy field? from whence then hath it tares? He said unto them, An enemy hath done this. The servants said unto him, Wilt thou then that we go and gather them up? But he said, Nay: lest while ye gather up the tares, ye root up also the wheat with them. Let both grow together until the harvest: and in the time of harvest I will say to the reapers, Gather ye together first the tares, and bind them in bundles to burn them: but gather the wheat into my barn.

In the gospel lesson for the Fifth Sunday after the Epiphany, a man sows seed in the field. Because of the evil act of an enemy, his labor is placed in jeopardy and he asks his Lord if he should do some weeding in order to correct the situation. The answer, I am sure, came as a suprise. He was told to do nothing until the harvest, and then the Lord Himself would take care of it by ordering the harvesters to make the necessary separation.

It is hard in the Christian life for most of us to decide what it is we must do and what it is we must allow God to do.

Too many of us see the Christian life as a lifelong struggle to reach an impossible perfection. We find ourselves struggling to purge ourselves of selfishness, enmity, and pettiness, and as we suffer one defeat after another, rail against God for setting before us such an impossible standard.

But God never said you had to do it alone—in fact, in today's lesson all He asks is that you plant. He, without your help, promises to remove the tares that blight your garden.

Jesus constantly warns us against taking up the fight against sin. He tells us about one man who did fight sin. He swept his house clean and got rid of the evil spirit that dwelt there. The empty house soon attracted seven spirits more evil than the first, and that man's last state was worse than the first.

What Jesus did tell us was to seek after the Kingdom of God and His righteousness first, and all the rest would be added unto us.

In short, by seeking after God and finding Him, the good life would come by His efforts. Do not then seek to become unselfish. Rather seek to find the incarnation of unselfishness, Jesus Christ. Do not seek to become less envious, less resentful, or less petty, but seek Him, who will make these things impossible in your life.

Too few people believe that the simple process of letting God in, will automatically drive all else out. But it is true, and each of us sooner or later must discover it. As we talk daily with Jesus and as we regularly frequent this table and sit in His Presence, our burden does become lighter.

Trust in Him and believe that He is present with you now, and in time you will find He has brought changes in your life, beyond your imagination.

Christ has promised not only to be present, but to come bearing the gift of the Spirit who brings life eternal and life more abundant.

When we come to the maturity of the harvest, God gathers us to Himself and destroys the tares in our lives, but the good seed which we ourselves have sown, He will gather into His house.

XI

THY FAITH HATH MADE THEE WHOLE

GOSPEL: LUKE: 17:19b

"Go thy way, Thy faith hath made thee whole."

How many times has Jesus said these words? "Thy faith hath made thee whole."

We read them throughout the gospels and yet the world doesn't get the message. Only after a dramatic experience did I really begin to appreciate what Jesus was trying to tell us in the above text. A few years ago as I drove into a small village to get gas, I saw a dramatic incident that brought the lesson home. As the attendant was filling my tank, I heard shouts and saw a man leave a house with another in hot pursuit. When the first man got into his car and drove off, the second in anger drove his fist through one of the windows in the house. The attendant ran into his store and called the police and then came out and shook his head and said, "He is full of wine again."

Later when I read the gospel lesson, the fact that came home to me was that this man's problems were due to something inside of him, but he was angry at someone else. What he was doing was what we all do so often, direct our anger towards someone or something outside of ourselves.

Most of our problems, if we can be honest with ourselves, lie within. We prefer to ignore this and blame someone or something. We cannot be made whole by changing others; we can only be made whole when we ourselves are filled with faith.

It is fashionable, I know, to blame society for a host of ills. And when I see angry young people bent on tearing society down, I wonder what is eating them inside. For surely, they like you and me are a part of this society, and if we want to make it better Jesus has shown us a way.

Individuals and societies can only become better through faith in God.

I say, if you see anything wrong with society, then change it. But change it, please, by beginning with yourself. This is the only part of society that you are in control of. And if you will turn to Christ and be made whole, your neighbor may be led to Christ and be made whole. And if enough people are made whole, society will be made whole.

The trouble with the world today is that we have a lot of people who want to make a better world by beginning with the other guy. Someone once said that when you point a finger at the other fellow, (illustrate) you are really pointing three fingers at yourself. I don't know any way to make this world better than by changing human lives, beginning with me.

Have you ever noticed that the Bible offers hope for the future to men and never to society as a whole. There are no promises for a new and more wonderful society. The promises are more direct and individual.

Christ offers **you** a new life; Christ offers **you** victory over death; Christ offers **you** an abundant life.

Society never responds to anything that anyone ever offers it. It only responds to human change. If people get worse, society gets worse, and if people get better, of course, our society will get better. A whole society is only possible when you and I become whole.

Even I, as your priest, can at this Mass only act for myself as I approach the Christ who is here present. You, and you alone, can give assent to receive Him in your heart. Whatever your reasons for being here, Jesus asks that you open your heart to receive Him, so that He can say to you. "Go thy way, Thy faith hath made thee whole."

XII

WHY HAVE YOU FORSAKEN ME?

PSALM 22:1

"My God, my God, why hast thou forsaken me? why art thou so far from helping me, and from the words of my roaring?"

The world is filled with people who feel that God has indeed forsaken them. Some are persons who have never had much to do with Him, but there are thousands of people whom we call religious who have turned away from Him because they are convinced He let them down. They often complain that when they needed Him most, they prayed, honestly and sincerely, and He failed to give them help.

When they bring their tale of woe to a pastor, he is at a loss as to what he should say. Sometimes years have elapsed since God's so-called failure, and it is difficult to fathom why the particular prayer was seemingly unanswered. I say seemingly because I have heard this cry of lament not only directed against God but often also directed against one's fellowman.

I remember vividly a young man who came into my study because he was convinced that I was his only friend. As he unfolded his tale of woe, it seemed that he had experienced one disappointment after another. His family did not care for him, and no one else seemed anxious to lend him a helping hand. "What was worse," he told me, "is that occasionally someone offered to help him, only to ultimately lose interest and cause him to experience one more disappointment. God, too, failed in so many critical times to answer his prayer.

The young man who came to see me was likeable and intelligent, and it seemed difficult to believe that I was his only friend. I tried to help him as best I could, but as I listened and observed, I discovered that almost no one had given up on the young man, and if he felt forsaken, it was all his own doing.

Oddly enough, he had reason to feel that people should turn their backs on him, for he had betrayed them and disappointed them again and again and again. In his self-pitying state he got himself in one jam after another, and each time he repeated the same pattern. Pretty soon he began to wonder if I would forsake him, and nothing I could say or do would convince him that I would not.

As we prayed together I discovered something else. He never really went to God. He didn't want to listen to God any more than he wanted to listen to me. He would come to me for advice, but he always knew in advance what he wanted to hear and what he was willing to accept. When he prayed he was never open to any answer that God might give him. He had an answer all picked out, and it is true that on that basis God did forsake him.

We so often come to God and ask Him to spare us the consequences of foolish and irresponsible acts.

A young man turns his back on God because his prayer is unanswered. He prayed that he might be able to meet a gambling debt he contracted without God's help. Another, that his girl friend is not pregnant as a consequence of something they did contrary to God's wishes and commandments. Another that his date of six months, whom he picked up in a bar, is not really married, as he now suspects. Another, that he does not have liver trouble that seems to be coming about as a result of years of intemperate living.

God will not forsake us in our times of trouble, but often he will not spare us from the consequences of our acts.

It does no good to plead that if He will only save us this time, we will not repeat our folly. For all too often we find ourselves in our present difficulty, precisely because we have in the past been able to avoid the evil consequences of our acts.

And as I recall the young man who pled that he was forsaken by everyone, including God, one thing sticks in my mind. When he used to come to see me, he never listened. He would ask for advice, and yet it was obvious that he had no capacity for listening.

I am sure he went to God in the same way, and I am equally sure that the day you felt God let you down, you were too overwrought to heed what he was trying to say to you.

It is trite but true that God is always more ready to speak to us than we are ready to listen.

What is true, "My God, my God, why hast thou forsaken me!" or should God say to you, "Man or woman, why have YOU forsaken ME?"

XIII

BE YE PERFECT

GOSPEL: MATTHEW 5:40-41

And if any man will sue thee at the law, and take away thy coat, let him have thy cloke also. And whosoever shall compel thee to go a mile, go with him twain.

As we read these very astonishing words of Jesus, we are so appalled at how much is demanded of us that we miss the purpose of the demand.

Peace overtures, like almost anything else, often fail because of halfhearted attempts, or halfway measures.

It is said that the principal cause of failure for a new business is under-capitalization. A man should invest 50,000, but because of fear of failure he invests only 40,000. The result is often failure, whereas the additional 10,000 would have changed failure into success.

We too often give of ourselves in the same halfhearted manner. We take a job but are fearful of giving too much of ourselves. We, perhaps, do a better job than anyone else in the office, but not enough better for the boss to notice, and hence our good work goes unrewarded.

Many people go about their Christian commitment in the same halfhearted way. God has a small portion of their loyalty. They give a little time, a little money, and a little of their love. Because God is their favorite charity, they expect to reap huge returns. But God is not mocked and will settle for nothing less than a total commitment to Him.

I know several churches with just under a hundred members that are failing to carry on an effective ministry in their communities. The members give just enough of themselves and their substance to keep the church alive, but not enough to make it effective. They therefore enjoy the dual privilege of boasting of their sacrifices while complaining of the shortcomings of the church and its ministry.

My father used to say that nothing was worth doing unless it was worth doing well. Or to put it another way, "No venture should be undertaken unless we are willing to put behind it the necessary resources and effort to see it through to a successful conclusion."

Whether you are going to begin something new, or whether you are going to patch up an old quarrel, Jesus' rule of going the second mile must be heeded.

Many times our apologies are refused and we find ourselves extremely resentful. Worse than that, the person we offended is more deeply hurt because of what he feels was a perfunctory, insincere attempt to patch up old differences.

We are too often like the child who says, "I am sorry, I guess."

Jesus doesn't guarantee that going the second mile will always work, but he strongly suggests that a willingness to go only one is apt to fail.

Christianity is not a faith for those who like to blow hot and cold. Jesus calls those, and only those, who will give heart and mind and soul in His service. And it is as if He would read our minds as we listen to the sermon on the mount, for He stops our protest by telling us,

"You, therefore, must be perfect, as your heavenly Father is perfect."

XIV
PEACE OF MIND

Several decades ago, Rabbi Liebmann wrote a book entitled *Peace of Mind*. Unintentionally he began a cult which enjoyed a great rage for over twenty years.

Americans had, at last, found a use for God. God was not some remote being in the heavens, but was the source of a most elusive quality of life, "Peace of Mind."

After that, all kinds of people began to discover that it was practical to believe in God. In fact, we even got one new sect that taught that if you really had faith, then your life would be blessed with health, wealth, and happiness. Those who failed to prosper, or whose joints ache with age, or rheumatism, obviously lacked faith. In short, people wanted to believe in God, because they felt it would pay off in the forms of all the good things of life.

Of all the forms of idolatry this is the most dangerous, since it is done in the Name of the One True God. Man never ceases creating gods in his own image, and hence it is difficult for us to decide Who is the True God and what can we expect from Him.

We can't say, "nothing," because one cannot come in contact with God without being profoundly affected.

Besides, Christ did promise us two results of faith. First, that we would have the abundant life, and secondly, that we would have life eternal.

Unfortunately the abundant life is the one that has been so distorted by the modern creators of idols. What did Christ mean by the abundant life? He possessed it, and yet He was a man of great sorrows. He possessed it, and yet He met death on the cross in his thirties.

But to others He gave every blessing. He healed the sick, brought the dead to life; and the Christians, who in the first century were poor, the enslaved, the destitute, became the rulers of the world.

The Christian is not one who receives great abundance, but **gives** great abundance.

A Christian does not spend his day counting his blessings, but in **being** a blessing to those about him. Wherever he goes lives are touched. He is the burden bearer of the world, and he sorrows for those who suffer, and yet the God that the Christian knows can heal, mend and restore.

Christ wept for Jerusalem because there were many who did not know God. This very act of caring brings sorrow to the hearts of all who love God and are concerned for his children.

Those who would measure the Christian life in terms of the benefits they would receive rather than the blessings they could bring to others fail to understand the gospel of Jesus Christ. They are idolaters because they do not love God or worship Him, but only what they can get their hands on. Their god consists of the things they seek from the Almighty, and they refuse to believe in a God that offers a life of service, of sorrow, in which the faithful must regard himself as the burden bearer of the meanest soul on earth.

Even life eternal is a gift that the idolaters would scorn, since **God,** not man, is central in the Heavenly Kingdom.

For what is Heaven but eternally dwelling in the presence of God! We shall dwell in the future life as we do here. Those who love God, and worship God, and for whom God is their friend and daily companion, **life will go on as it is.** For Jesus truly said, the kingdom of Heaven is among you.

But for those whose god is found among transient things, the future holds no more than it does for all things material. Surely moth and rust will corrupt the treasures which they so naively attribute to God.

They have those things which God has created, and in acquiring them, they have missed the best part.

The true Christian seeks after God for His own sake. Because God loved Him, gave him life, and daily blesses Him, the Christian seeks Him out to render thanks.

Here are some simple things that God **does do** for you.

First, He has given, nay, continues to give you life.

Second, He permits you to come into His presence. This is a great blessing, for it allows us

1. to render thanks. How dreadful it would be to receive life and all these good things and to be able to offer nothing in return. We can, and we should give thanks daily.

2. We need to come into His presence to ask forgiveness. Mistakes come so easily, and to bear them without being able to unburden our souls would be a great weight. But we can come to God, confess our faults and receive His forgiveness.

3. We need to seek His guidance. It seems strange that so many find the world so difficult to live in and yet never once ask the creator of the world "How best to live in it." God can guide our lives and help us choose our vocations, and at every crossroads help us to make the right decision.

Finally, who can come in the presence of God and not wish to sing His praises? Those who do not worship are truly in darkness, for the most elementary knowledge of God, the most fleeting glimpse, provokes in man the desire to sing praises to His Name.

In short, God does do many things for you because He loves you. I am sure you can not, and dare not, seek to use God. You must serve Him for the same reason He serves you, because you love Him.

Only then will your life have meaning and purpose—only then will your thoughts be lifted from a petty and self-defeating concern for yourself to a life of service to God and to others.

For Jesus has truly said that "He who would save his life shall surely lose it, but he who would lose his life for my sake and the gospel's shall surely find it."

XV

SIMON THE CYRENIAN

GOSPEL: LUKE 23:26

And as they led him away, they laid hold upon one Simon, a Cyrenian, coming out of the country, and on him they laid the cross, that he might bear it after Jesus.

When we decide to obey God we receive a whole host of benefits, and in time we share them with others. Our obedience to God makes us easier to live with having more generous feelings towards others, and we become one of those who seek to give more than he receives. But by the same token, our obedience to God oftentimes costs others more than it costs us.

If we are in love with God, obedience to Him costs us nothing, for it is a delight to do his will. But if we obey God, it means that other people's plans will be upset. An innocent like Simon comes along and must bear a cross he never sought.

Many a man thought he would never have a problem being faithful, until being faithful brought threats to his family.

Those behind the iron curtain who still choose to attend church bring penalties, not upon themselves alone, but upon their families. And what if their families do not believe? They become upset and gibe us with, "How can you allow this to happen to us and call yourself Christian?"

We have seen children curse their parents because they blame the pogroms, not upon the sinfulness of others, but because of their heritage. Only too late, did some of them see the folly of denying their heritage.

But in our own pride, we often want to be obedient to God, providing we alone can bear the cost. We say we will bear every cost, any humiliation, but we want to do it alone.

Yet you cannot dictate to God how you will obey Him. And you cannot shelter others from the consequences of the good that you do anymore than you can shelter them from the consequences of the evil that you may do.

For in a sense, we and our families are held hostage in an evil world. Those who would have us be dishonest will whisper in our ears that to do otherwise will deprive our families of so much. They would have us believe, that we would be willing to commit sins for the sake of others, that we would not for ourselves.

And so the publisher of pornography, the peddler of drugs, and the bookie, all plead that obedience to God would place the cross of poverty upon their families and their dependents.

It is a strange contradiction, because these people, like ourselves, gave little thought to the cross that disobedience must have placed upon the shoulders of each and everyone of their loved ones.

I have known of children who had difficulty explaining their father's business to their playmates. I have known fathers who feared that their children might be caught in the same nefarious trade they pursued. And it was all done in the rationalization that "I must provide for my family." Perhaps, our problem comes in that we see only one cross when in reality there are many.

There is the cross upon which the thieves on either side of Jesus hung. It comes because of the evil we do, and like the other cross, it is borne not only by ourselves, but by all those who share our lives. The boy who goes to jail may not suffer nearly so much as his mother, who grieves at home. The ostracism that comes to the illegal bookie hurts him not nearly so much as his college-age daughter.

If we ask others to bear these crosses, which are symbols of the evil we do, why not ask them to bear aloft with us the crosses that symbolize the good that we do.

A dentist in a small Illinois community exposed the corrupt officials of the town in which he lived. He lost his practice, and both he and his family bore the cross of social ostracism. However, they bore it proudly and willingly.

Whatever choice we make in this world, we must leave the consequences to God. We do not live alone, and everything we do is somehow shared with others. Hence, our choice must be based on our love for God. When we willingly obey Him, we cannot dictate to Him what we will allow to happen as the result of our obedience. Each of us must be prepared to bear our cross and pray that those who are near and dear to us will willingly assume their burdens as God gently places them upon their shoulders.

In His House

XVI
THE FELLOWSHIP OF CHRIST

GOSPEL: MATTHEW 3:13-17

Then cometh Jesus from Galilee to Jordon unto John, to be baptized of him. But John forbad him, saying, I have need to be baptized of thee, and comest thou to me? And Jesus answering said unto him, Suffer it to be so now: for thus it becometh us to fulfil all righteousness. Then he suffered him. And Jesus, when he was baptized, went up straightway out of the water: and, lo, the heavens were opened unto him, and he saw the Spirit of God descending like a dove, and lighting upon him: And lo a voice from heaven, saying, This is my beloved Son, in whom I am well pleased.

Some years ago in St. Catherine's parish, where I taught, the new rules on baptism were introduced. It is nice to note that the role of the parents is somewhat larger in the new liturgy than the old. But in going over it, I felt quite disappointed. It seems to me that two very central facts concerning the baptism of Jesus failed to receive sufficient emphasis.

It is good to know that infant baptism is a dedication of a child to God. We need, of course, to be reminded of how great and yet how limited our responsibility is. As parents and sponsors, we cannot help but be conscious of the fact that it is no easy matter to rear a child and to train him in the ways of the Lord. We can teach him the Commandments, we can teach him how to pray, and provide for his instruction in the Christian faith. But when the day for his confirmation arrives, his future is in his own hands. At that moment he must decide. All—parents, priest, sponsors and faithful members of the church must passively wait to see if the child whom they once pledged to God will pick up his responsibilities and choose to serve Christ.

It is true that in the new rite, as in the old, it is crystal clear that this is a dedication to God. And yet, I am fearful that many will continue to view it as primarily a commitment to the church. I hope not, for the world is filled with people who are committed to this cause, to that movement, to this or that nation, or even to this or that religious denomination. The unique thing about Christian baptism is that it is not primarily a commitment to ANY THING, but a commitment to a person. For unless men and women are committed to God, and to His service, they have missed the point of living.

At the heart of the Christian gospel is the simple message that we live for Him who gave us life—the Almighty God, our Creator and Redeemer.

Secondly, I would have liked to have seen in the new rite more emphasis of the role of God at baptism.

It is good to be made aware of what it is that we are doing, as we bring a child to receive this Sacrament. But unless we realize that God is coming to us and that we stand in His presence, the act of baptism will be more human than divine. After all, it is God's imminent presence that gives baptism its sacramental character.

John questioned Jesus concerning his need for baptism, but Jesus shrugged aside his objections. What John was overlooking was the blessing of God, the Father, which takes place in every true and valid baptism. We come to offer our feeble words of dedication, but we come also to hear God's promise to us, that we are His sons and daughters and heirs to His Kingdom. For baptism is not to be thought of as a rite, or even a dedication, but as a moment when God and man come together to pledge their mutual love for one another.

As this child was received today in our midst, I pray that each and everyone of us here has renewed his pledge of his love to God and prepared his heart to receive God's love and God's blessing.

XVII

PENTECOST

The Day of Pentecost brought home forcibly to the apostles how tightly they were bound together. The events of Good Friday, Easter and the Ascension had not loosened, but tightened the bonds of fellowship. From this day forth they would share all of the blessings and the risks of the Christian communion.

Like Christ, they would risk betrayal by an occasional Judas, disappointment by a Peter that might deny them, and they would carry untold burdens for the lame and the blind and the halt among them. They would do so out of love, a love born in them through Christ who gave them His love beyond measure.

All these things they would do because the Spirit gave them utterance and the Spirit gave them strength. Because of it, they would grow closer to one another and closer to God.

All this sounds so ideal, and yet in practice it is so real.

Chiara Lubich tells of a visit to a friend in a hospital. A man was in a plaster cast. "His chest and one arm, the right arm, were in plaster. With his left, he tried to do everything as best he could. The cast was a torture for him, but the left arm, while it was tired out by the end of the day, grew more robust by doing the work of two."

In the same way we as members of the church are often called to carry the burdens that others should be doing. But when they can't, we grow strong. We sometimes wonder, and sometimes even resent, being burden bearers, but it is we who benefit; it is we who grow strong. A good church fellowship must always include those who are spiritually strong, together with the weak. Each is needed, and each contributes to the strengthening of the other.

Christians never ask whether or not they are givers or receivers. For God has in a wonderful way made it possible for him who receives, to give, and for him who gives, to receive the wonderful gift of strengthening.

The Holy Spirit came not alone into Peter's heart, but touched those who heard and those who gave utterance.

We are one great fellowship in Christ. He is the strength in our midst and He gathers the rich and the poor, the sighted and the sightless, the strong and the weak. Together we serve God, never stopping to count our burdens, but rather stopping often to give thanks for those things which we receive and for the opportunities to give service that are for our enrichment, even as we strive to make others rich.

XVIII

FRIENDS OF JESUS

GOSPEL: JOHN 15:14

"Ye are my friends, if ye do whatsoever I command you."

Who are they who are called to be members of the Church of Christ? Jesus says, they are his friends.

Perhaps in a sense, the essence of church membership is that we have declared ourselves to be friends of Jesus. For friendship with Him is different from any other friendship that we have known. It does have some of the same ingredients of ordinary friendship. Jesus says that a true friend would lay down his life for his brother. It also affords us the fellowship and the companionship that we all so greatly need.

But unlike other friendships which say, "I will give you all, but don't try to tell me what I must do," Jesus says, "You are my friends, if you do whatsoever, I command you."

Here is an important difference. Our profession of love and friendship must also be a profession of obedience to his will. For Christ offers us something no other friend can offer. He knows our needs better than we do ourselves. When I wish to bend your will to mine, no matter how often I protest that I seek your ultimate good, there exists the probability that I am seeking only to satisfy my own needs and to further my own good.

But Christ knows us and knows better than we do what is for our own good. He is the one friend in whom we can place our lives and know that we will receive direction that will give us all that we need or desire.

It is for this reason that He says we have not chosen Him, but He has chosen us and ordained us to go forth in His name.

No man dare permit another man to use Him, precisely because he has already been committed to Christ's use. Since God would use us for His heavenly purposes, we cannot allow ourselves to be used by others.

You are my friends," says Jesus, "if you do whatsoever I command you."

You have assured yourselves of this friendship by your profession of obedience. For all are friends of Christ who are pledged to do His will.

It ought to be a pledge easily given, for Christ does have a plan for our lives. He alone knows us well enough to make our lives truly count. By giving ourselves to His will, we are assured that He will watch over our every step, not so much that He fears we shall fall, but that we may receive the good things He has reserved for us.

For a life in Christ, as the early apostles discovered, is an adventurous life, filled with blessings for those who love the things of God. Jesus said, "I have come that you might have life eternal and life more abundant." And this promise He will surely keep for those who love Him and do His will.

XIX

PRAYING FOR THE PEOPLE OF GOD

GOSPEL JOHN: 17:9

I pray for them; I pray not for the world, but for them which thou has given me; for they are mine."

Jesus prays only for those whom God has given Him. Not because He does not love others, not because he has no concern for them, but because He has no basis for prayer.

It would be foolish to believe that God would do something for Joe Doaks only because you spoke in his behalf. But God does answer our prayers on behalf of ourselves and for those who are part of His mystical Body. It is only logical that He should, for He has asked us to bear one another's burdens and to unite ourselves in His Body here on earth.

Hence, when we pray for our brothers and sisters, we are, in effect, praying also for ourselves. God does not ask me to become part of you, and then wash His hands of the affair. By uniting myself with you I may be lifted up to the highest that is in you, or I may be brought down to the lowest that is in you. Consequently, when I offer my prayers to Him to keep you from stumbling, I am praying also in my own behalf.

A Christian offers his prayer in the plural, for God has placed him in the fellowship of his fellow beings. Because we stand and fall together, we offer our supplications together, and the blessings are bestowed upon us as a Christian family.

Christians share together, not only of their material resources, but also of their spiritual resources. God is not my God, but He is truly **our** Father.

We may, with faith, pray for all those with whom we share any portion of our lives. The truly committed Christian may freely give of himself, knowing that God will answer not only our prayers for ourselves, but also for those He has sent to us.

You must pray for all those to whom you are bound, for if God does not lift you up together, you will not be able to carry the burdens you have assumed.

XX

WALKING IN THE SPIRIT

EPISTLE: GALATIANS 5:25

"If we live in the Spirit, let us also walk in the Spirit."

St. Paul, in his letter to the Galatians, tries to bring faith and works together. He is convinced that no man can live by the law unless the Holy Spirit helps him. He is also convinced that faith that does not result in good works is worthless.

I can still remember the discussions in my childhood confirmation class over the relative importance of faith and works.

If I remember correctly we seem to have missed the central point that Paul was trying to make. A few years later there was a popular song that in a strange manner clarified it for me. You may recall it. The lines went like this, "Love and marriage, love and marriage, you can't have one without the other." Faith and works go together in much the same way. Too many people today underestimate the value of religious instruction.

A few years ago, a man in Manchester discovered dollar bills flying around on the street. As he gathered them together he found a bag that had been broken open, containing several hundred dollars. How anyone would react in that kind of situation depends on many factors. Many would keep the money, and probably as many would return it to its rightful owner.

If I were to venture an opinion on why many people would act honestly, I would say it was because they had decided in advance how they would act under those circumstances. Children and adults need to study and learn what Christians believe about honesty, purity, unselfishness, and love.

A lot of people today think that they can decide such questions as they arise. They believe they do not need to send their children to church school because they can teach them right and wrong at home. Home training is most essential but it is usually not enough. You can teach your children reading, writing, and arithmetic at home too, but you don't, primarily because it is too big a job. Yet it isn't half so big as teaching righteous behavior.

A boy or girl has to know not only that he ought to be honest, but he actually has to think about situations which might confront him. A lot of parents tell their children they ought to be honest, and then boast at the dinner table about some fast deal they made. Or Dad brings home tools from the plant and mother supplies the children with pencils, paper and erasers she has stolen from the office. When you are given too much change, whether you keep it or give it back depends on your belief about honesty. You don't decide at the time—you have already decided that days, weeks, years in advance.

Time and time again in confessions people talk about not sins but mistakes. It took me quite a while to learn the distinction. A sin, I learned, is something you plan in advance, while a mistake is some wrong you did on the spur of the moment. The trouble is that our belief determines in advance What we do on the spur of the moment.

For example, if you read Ann Landers' column you probably have noticed the number of young people who write and ask why it is not permissible for them as couples to take distant trips together. Ann Landers does a pretty good job at telling them, but we can be sure some don't listen. Others don't even write. When such trips end unfortunately, the couples will think they made a mistake, little realizing that they planned it all in advance. No man or woman puts himself or herself deliberately in a situation where he is apt to make a mistake.

XXI
THE LORD HAS NEED OF US

I SAMUEL 3:10

And the Lord came, and stood, and called as at other times, "Samuel, Samuel." Then Samuel answered, "Speak; for thy servant heareth."

Committed Christian people are anxious to follow the leading of God's Holy Spirit. Unfortunately, for most of us, it seems, at times, a difficult thing to do. The saints seem to differ as to whether we should quietly wait for God's guidance, or whether we should immerse ourselves in activity while we are waiting to hear.

We are confronted with a paradox, for most of the significant things which God revealed to the saints came to them in a moment when they were engaged in some activity. Yet, time and time again God cautions us not to lose ourselves in the cares of this world.

On the other hand we have seen the danger of "quietism" where people spent countless hours in quiet inactivity waiting for the Spirit to speak to them. This often leads to a desire for the dramatic and the avoidance of the many seemingly simple things that God requires of us.

It is a mistake to regard activity, per se, as bad. In Samuel's words to God lies the key to the question of how can we be sure of hearing the Holy Spirit. It is the servant who hears. Ten men can be working, but only one hears his master's voice. He who is the servant of the master hears when his master speaks.

Often our activity is a form of escape, and if it is, we shall be successful. Neither quietism brings us the Holy Spirit, nor activity, if we are not the servants of the Lord.

It is difficult to see how inactive man can regard himself as God's servant, for God demands of us first of all that we embrace life, and life is almost synonymous with activity. Nor can the man who labors for himself and for his own ends regard himself as a servant. But he who seeks to do the will of the Lord will always be ready to hear. For the work becomes not an end in itself, but is only another service to be performed until the Master requires something else. Then it is easy for a true servant to drop what he is doing and begin a new task with enthusiasm.

A good measure of our commitment is the ease at which we can switch from one God-given task to another. If we rebel when we are called to new forms of service, it may be that the work we have been doing has been for our own ends and for our own personal satisfaction.

This is the clue to the nature of our commitment. For the servant seeks only to please the master, and each new call to service brings pleasure. For what greater compliment can we receive, but that the Lord hath need of us.

Pitfalls of the Spiritual Life

XXII

THE PITFALLS OF THE SPIRITUAL LIFE

Some time ago, I heard a preacher summarize all the advantages of the Christian life. First, Church members live, on the average, many years longer than non-Church people. Secondly, an astonishing number of their marriages are successful in an age when non-Church people are recording one out of three marriages as failures. Crime, one out of three marriages as failures. Crime, drugs, alcoholism are not unknown to Christian homes, but the incidence is so rare we seem to be talking about a different race of people. When he got done, I almost asked aloud if the Christian life didn't have some hazards of its own.

The first is rather obvious. In the face of what I have just said, it is easy for a Christian to become smug and proud. That we have been blessed is without question; whether we are worthy of it is something on which we should reflect.

A second hazard is a tendency to become rather insular. Christians spend so much time talking to Christians that they lose the ability to communicate with those who have no faith. Sometimes we monder why it is that we make so little impact upon the world about us.

I remember a friend many years back who was telling me about the hard-hitting sermons he preached. He took particular pride in the claim that he spoke without fearing any man's criticism. One of the sermons that he thought was particularly courageous was one that hit the liquor traffic hard. His entire congregation was made up of teetotalers, and there wasn't a soul in the church that didn't applaud his very "courageous" word. In a way it was fortunate that none of the town drunks went to his church. The sermon wouldn't have convinced any of them, because he never talked with any of them, and he did not know people of this type well enough to be able to reach them.

Many of us are in this predicament. Either we don't have sufficient contact with persons without faith, or if we do, we speak such a different language theat we can't communicate our deepest and most vital convictions.

Finally, there is a tendency not to care enough. We are like some rich who struggled to climb the ladder and are not only indifferent to the poor, but critical because they didn't struggle as hard and as successfully as they.

Because we know that with a little effort our neighbors could find God, and because we feel there is nothing we can do anyway, so why should we try. But the age old challenge is there. I am my brother's keeper, and to whom much has been given shall much be required.

The pitfalls of the spiritual life are many, but these three stand out.

We dare not lose ourselves in pride.

We dare not lose our brother by withdrawing from his world.

Nor may we be anymore indifferent to our neighbor's spiritual needs, than to his material needs, and as we would not let him physically starve, so likewise we cannot stand by and let him spiritually starve.

We should examine our own effectiveness and pray that God will take away whatever stands in the way of our reaching people, whether it be our indifference, our isolation, or our pride.

"To God be all glory in His creation, now and forever."

XXIII

BE THANKFUL

JEREMIAH 2:2

Go and cry in the ears of Jerusalem, saying, Thus saith the Lord; I remember thee, the kindness of thy youth, the love of thine espousals, when thou wentest after me in the wilderness, in a land that was not sown.

What does God mean when He says that He remembers the kindness of our youth? Isn't He calling attention to the fact that so many of us no longer have the enthusiasm for God that we once had?

With the first discovery of God each person's life seems to be marked by a zeal that passes away in time. In this encounter with Jeremiah, God is bemoaning the fact that this is so.

I am sure that at times each and everyone of us thinks back to a time when his or her faith reached a mountaintop experience. Yet, if we find ourselves nostalgic about what our faith used to be, we need to ask ourselves why we no longer experience the same zeal and enthusiasm of our youth.

In part, this is due to the fact that many of us have become tired. In our younger days we seemed to have boundless energy and were anxious to use it all in the service of God. Now, in our riper years we sometimes feel a need to conserve energy, and we are no longer anxious to lift new burdens. Perhaps we need to be reminded that God never asks us to do more than we are able.

Secondly, we have become blasé. We no longer expect to have God lead us to new experiences and new adventures. It is becoming increasingly true that at a very early age that we tend to think we have seen and experienced everything. It is amazing that the same group of young people that rushes headlong to taste of every experience and is so fearful lest something be missed that it wishes to include even drugs, so quickly tires and refuses to consider new challenges and new adventures.

Not too long ago I asked a group of high school students whether they would like to spend a summer in Europe, and over half indicated no interest whatsoever. It was not that they had had this experience, but they viewed it as merely another experience in a world filled with real and vicarious experiences, via TV, easy travel, and premature exposure to experiences another generation would have saved for maturity.

And yet God does open up new doors and new opportunities to all who will follow his Holy Spirit. It is amazing how many of the followers of Christ are people who have first come to know Him in their old age. I think of the late Canon Streeter who in his last years was convinced he had written his last book and taken on his last adventure. Then God touched his life, and life seemed to have a new beginning, filled with the same excitement and adventure of his youth.

I remember a woman in her seventies who began a missionary career that took her from one end of this country to another. I remember a retired insurance man who began a new career in religious art, and in his last years created the only enduring work of his life.

Finally, even the most wonderful things of life are taken for granted, unless we strive to keep our wonder alive.

I once lived in a very scenic part of Maine and soon discovered that the natives never saw the sunsets and never really looked at the hundreds of breathtaking views. They were more excited by a photo of the Rockies, which they had never seen, than the first hand views which surrounded them on every side.

A Christian must keep alive his faith and the wonder of it by constantly re-viewing the blessings of God.

Just recently, I have tried to help three young people whose lives were threatened because they felt alone and forsaken. It has made me more mindful of the wonderful way in which God has blessed me; first of all by His own care, and secondly by giving me a family that loves me, and finally, by setting me here in the midst of this fellowship with whom I can share my joys and sorrows.

If we remember the security with which God surrounds us, His daily blessings, both material and spiritual, and finally, the assurance He brings us of life abundant and life eternal, the faith we have today will exceed the faith of our youth. May God help you, not only to preserve your faith, but through your acts of daily thanksgiving enable your faith to grow!

XXIV

FAITH IN TURBULENT TIMES

EPISTLE: ROMANS 8:31-39

What shall we then say to these things? If God be for us, who can be against us He that spared not his own Son, but delivered him up for us all, how shall he not with him also freely give us all things? Who shall lay anything to the charge of God's elect? It is God that justifieth. Who is he that condemneth? It is Christ that died, yea rather, that is risen again, who is even at the right hand of God, who also maketh intercession for us.
Who shall separate us from the love of Christ? shall tribulation, or distress, or persecution, or famine, or nakedness, or peril, or sword? As it is written, For thy sake we are killed all the day long; we are accounted as sheep for the slaughter. Nay, in all these things we are more than conquerors through him that loved us. For I am persuaded, that neither death, nor life, nor angels, nor principalities, nor powers, nor things present, nor things to come. Nor height, nor depth, nor any other creature, shall be able to separate us from the love of God, which is in Christ Jesus our Lord.

It is a wonderful thing that the church had its beginning in times as turbulent as our own. Because it prospered in violent times, we can take heart and have hope that it will be equally victorious in our day.

Make no mistakes, the church today is under attack, as it has never been since St. Paul's day. Only a few decades ago, none of the media would publish cartoons which depicted clergymen, lest someone take offense. I, along with many of you, welcomed Brother Juniper, and a whole host of cartoons which seemed to make the clergy and the church seem more human and real.

Maybe you haven't noticed, but on T.V. and in the so-called sophisticated magazines, the humor is no longer warm and friendly, but often malicious and angry.

A movement is underway to tax the churches and the many charitable institutions they operate. In Kansas they have already begun taxing the Rectories. Even if you believe that the church buildings should be taxed, you must recognize the fact that many of the leaders of the movement are enemies of the church. Knowing that the power to tax is the power to destroy, they hope to weaken the church by using the arm of the government. However, the great threat to the churches does not come from without, but from within.

The biggest threat comes from those who desire to usher in what they falsely believe to be the Kingdom of God, by mobilizing the church's power and going into the market place. They hope by social change to create a world which they believe is more just, more peaceful and more godly. Unfortunately, they seem to have forgotten the way of Jesus Christ.

For if there is one thing the church does not have it is power. Christ left his disciples nothing in the way of political or social power. What he gave the church was the gift of himself. And if we are to remake men and nations, it is going to have to be through the love of Christ. Christ did not give us power to coerce, but he gave His love to win all men unto him.

Among those who would weaken the church are the fearful, who are afraid to preach the gospel once handed down to the apostles, because it does not seem modern enough for our age. The advocates of the new morality quite rightly say that situations alter our moral code. What they fail to say is that there are times when we must be more loving, more unselfish, and more sacrificing than others. Never does Christ permit us to put aside our love, dilute our purity, or become just a little bit selfish.

The one prevailing bigotry in our world today is the dogmatic assertion that there are no absolutes. The Christ who died upon Calvary's Cross believed in love and love absolutely.

What shall we then say to these things? Christ has shown us the way and has promised through Paul that we shall conquer. But, let us not deceive ourselves. We shall not conquer except by the love of Christ.

If we believe that we can erect new and elaborate church structures that will defeat those forces which assail the church from within and without, we think foolishly. The victory Christ has promised comes only when we give ourselves in total and complete commitment to Him, Who alone gives us victory.

Nor can we hope to save ourselves and our world by adherence to the old liturgies, regardless of their beauty and their worth. The Roman catholic nostagically praying for the return of the Latin Mass or the Anglican clutching his Book of Common Prayer cannot assure us the victory. These things have value, to be sure, and I love the insurpassable beauty of morning prayer, but they are not central except when they aid us in coming to Christ and making a more perfect commitment to Him.

Among Old Catholics there seems to be a conviction almost bordering on superstition that we can frighten the devil and his hordes, if only we can get together enough prelates in fancy robes and even more elaborate titles and celebrate a super Mass.

I assume that those who are gathered here this evening are not numbered among the enemies of the church, within or without. I am not so sure that all of us at one time or another do not fall victim to some of the falacious ways we sometimes choose to defend Christ and His Church.

Fortunately, in our better moments we know that there are no substitutes and no short cuts. Nothing will suffice except Paul's injunction that we present ourselves unto Christ as a living sacrifice. This alone is acceptable and pleasing to God.

If you believe that the way out of our dilemna lies in a recommitment to Christ and His Church, then I have not come this distance in vain. For on the basis of three Catholic truths can we together meet the challenge to Christ and His Church.

First, that we do not stand alone as His defenders. Christ is His own best defender, and He is present in this world. Christians who are truly committed to Him have no trouble finding Him. Even as we strive to dwell in Him, He dwells in us. He is ever present at the celebration of the Mass, and He is our rock and our fortress in the midst of the turmoil of the world.

Secondly, as Catholics, we believe it is necessary to regularly come into his presence, in order that we might know His will in our lives and receive from His presence the strength to obey. For it is not as princes and rulers that we shall prevail, but as servants of the suffering Christ.

And finally, if you believe that men and society can be transformed by the renewing power of the gospel, there is hope that we shall together help build His Kingdom.

The church has managed to prevail in many critical times, but only when men and women have given themselves completely to Him and to His Service.

If we believe that Christ lives in the midst of His Church, if we are willing to give ourselves to Him, and if we will serve Him in the task of proclaiming the gospel without compromise, then we too shall be persuaded that neither death, nor life, nor angels, nor principalities, nor powers, nor things present, nor things to come, nor height, nor depth, nor any other creature shall be able to separate us from the love of God, which is in Christ Jesus our Lord.

XXV

WE ARE STRANGERS IN THIS WORLD

I PETER 2:11

Dearly beloved, I beseech you as strangers and pilgrims, abstain from fleshy lusts, which war against the soul.

Almost from the day man is born he knows that he is called to another world. The thing that distinguishes man from the beasts is the fact that man alone worships God.

Only man finds the world too small; only man is unwilling to believe that life can be contained in three score years and ten. Only man believes that the world of the spirit is to be preferred over the material world of the flesh.

Unfortunately as Wordsworth so aptly put it, the "world is too much with us," and we often find our faith in the hereafter wavering as we are confronted with the problems of the here and now.

Yet Peter calls us to the correct posture when he tells us we must regard ourselves as strangers and pilgrims.

The gospels give us sufficient direction to avoid three pitfalls in dealing with the world outside the church.

First we cannot forget that even as strangers and pilgrims, we do live in the world. Even as strangers we have some responsibilities, if only to give witness to others concerning our motives and intentions.

The Christian cannot ignore the world's need. He must give alms, and above all, he must preach the gospel and seek to win men to God. On the Christian heart is placed a tremendous concern for the need of all mankind. But note that the concern is largely other than worldly.

While Jesus went about healing the sick of body, He was primarily concerned with the sick of soul.

He was not indifferent to the segregated Samaritans. In fact, He associated with them freely and directly and indirectly He pleaded their cause. But it was difficult to imagine Jesus working to get the Samaritan or the modern Negro, into some segregated club only to have him wind up in an integrated hell.

No, as Christians, we cannot be self-centered. We need to give alms, to do what we can to alleviate physical suffering.

But this is not our purpose in the world, and it can never be all there is to the Christian gospel. Those who would make civil rights the beginning and end-all of the gospel must believe that God is only the god of this world. But Jesus reminded us that His kingdom was not of this world, and it is the other world that takes priority.

What are three score years and ten compared to an eternity?

We are truly pilgrims and strangers seeking to find God in this world and seeking to find ourselves. It is a place of preparation where we learn to live in peace with one another. Oddly enough we can only do this when we renounce the world and all that it stands for. For men have never quarreled over spiritual things, but over the material things of the world. The so-called religious wars are misnamed, for men fought for earthly kingdoms and material possessions.

History has shown us three stages of the Church.

One is illustrated by the tremendous castle in the ancient city of Salzburg that once belonged to the archbishop. When my wife and I visited it some time ago, I thought she would be impressed with the wealth of the archbishop. I expected to hear harsh words of criticism about vows of poverty and simplicity and the obvious extravagant and conspicous spending. But the castle had some even harsher examples of worldly concerns, a torture chamber equipped with devices that no Christian could condone and remain a Christian.

This is the self-centered view that perhaps conceives God as totally other worldly. We are now witnessing the opposite extreme. God, we are told, is dead to the other world, and lives, if He lives at all, only in this world.

If heaven exists at all, it must be created here and now. God's law is to be imposed upon the world by people who cannot even rule themselves. So anxious are they to bring God in this world that they insist upon bringing Him down to the level of man.

If this generation cannot understand the music of the angels, then God must be taught to understand rock and roll. If this generation cannot learn to worship God in beauty and holiness, then God must come to them in chaos, confusion and filth.

I once witnessed a so-called rock and roll Mass that apparently assumed that cleanliness and filth were equal in the sight of God. I am sure God would not stop an unwashed person from coming to Him, but I am equally sure that an unwashed person, who knew he was in the presence of God, would soon feel uncomfortable until he had become clean.

In the same manner sinners are invited to come to God, but you can be sure that if they remain sinners, they are not aware of the fact that they are in God's presence or they are completely unregenerate and unsaved.

No, God is the God of two worlds. He is in this earth, and He bids us follow Him to His world up above. He never comes down to us, but seeks to raise us up to Him.

Do not ask us to tailer the Church Catholic to the world, for we shall remain faithful to our commitment to shape the world according to the Church Catholic.

Do not tell us times have changed and therefore the church should change. For if times have changed and the world has not, then we shall only renew our efforts to change the world until it resembles Christ's Kingdom.

For Christ has a kingdom on this earth. Remember how it began, with twelve disciples, and one was named Judas. It was perfectly integrated, but Christ promised that before the end it would be segregated, and the sheep would go into one fold and the goats into another.

So let me remind you that you are strangers and pilgrims in this world. As you go through, give alms, feed the poor, visit the prisoner, clothe the naked; above all do not neglect to proclaim the gospel that we are called to His Heavenly Kingdom.

XXVI

THE ENIGMA OF THE CROSS

I CORINTHIANS 1:23-24

> But we preach Christ crucified, unto the Jews a stumbling block, and unto the Greeks foolishness; but unto them which are called both Jews and Greeks, Christ the power of God, and the wisdom of God.

The cross is an enigma, i.e., a riddle, for the so-called practical people of the world. It is a riddle for the sentimentalists who cry, "Why must there be pain and sorrow in the world?" It is a riddle for those who would order the world in such a fashion as to demand no sacrifices, no great labor, and never a price to be paid for anything.

Napoleon Bonaparte was just such a realist. As a consequence he had no use for the church and understood nothing that she stood for. As an opponent of the church, he hoped to rid France of this institution. He shared his ideas with one of his advisors and said flatly that he wanted him to think of a new religion to take the place of the Catholic church. The reply came immediately, and the advisor said they could begin whenever Napoleon wished. "All we have to do," the advisor said, "is to kill someone, and then have him rise from the dead, on the third day."

Napoleon had not reckoned on the cross. For the people of France were attracted, not to some religion of fables nor a religion of rules for good behaviour, but to the reality of the cross and Christ's victory over the cross.

What is the attraction of the cross? First the cross represents the price we pay for sin. It is a harsh, unpleasant, and disagreeable fact. But it is a fact that man suffers as a consequence of his sin and the collective sin of all mankind.

We often fail to see the connection between our sufferings and sin, because often the suffering comes long after or seems to have no direct bearing upon the sins of our youth. If Christ took upon himself the sins of all mankind, so it seems that often you and I must take upon ourselves the sins of all mankind.

The child who dies in a bombing raid in Viet Nam may be sinless, but he, even as an infant, must bear part of the burden of the world's sin. The victim of an accident caused by a drunken driver becomes a burden bearer carrying his share of the pain of sin. Practical people, realistic people—people with both feet on the ground do not overlook this reality of life.

But this cross is not just a price, but also a reconciliation. Here in the midst of settling our accounts, we face the Lord of the accounts. It takes a brave man, indeed, to seek anything from someone to whom he owes much. Many of us do not seek God nor desire to be in His presence, for we feel there is much to settle between us.

But Christ has led the way. For He did not deem Himself too great to take upon Himself the burdens of all mankind. The astonishing effect was to lift him up to the father. When we are ready to willingly take up our cross, not for our sakes, but for the sake of our brother, we shall be reconciled to God.

This reconciliation brings the final victory which so frustrated Napoleon. The cross represents not only Christ's ransom for sin, his reconciliation with God, the Father, but victory over the grave.

For, however hard the way, the reward is beyond our comprehension. Yet it is simple to understand, for life eternal is a life in the presence of God and all that it implies. It is only when we have come to love the things that God loves that His presence seems inviting. For those who love God, and who willingly bear the cross, Christ has promised life and life eternal. This is the one love that goes forever. Learn to love the Lord God today, and you will dwell in His love forever.

XXVII
COUNTING THE COST

GOSPEL: LUKE 14:28-30

For which of you, intending to build a tower, sitteth not down first, and counteth the cost, whether he have suficient to finish it? Lest haply after he hath laid the foundation, and is not able to finish it, all that behold it begin to mock him. Saying, This man began to build, and was not able to finish.

All my life I have been told that the Christian attitude was **not** to count the cost. Yet, time and time again, we see Jesus cautioning men lest they decide to follow him before they have weighed the cost.

Jesus is not anxious to mislead men into believing that it would be easy to follow him. He is not anxious to have men start out in an undertaking which they cannot or will not finish.

One time, he even told a parable where he said it was better to go all out after the mammon of unrighteousness than to give a half-hearted allegiance to God and a half-hearted allegiance to the devil.

To follow Christ Jesus demands that we count the cost before we begin.

First of all He would have us know that no man can serve two masters. Sooner or later, if we persist in following Him, the world will reject us.

Many people labor under the delusion that they can go to Church on Sunday and spend the rest of the week in constant company of non-Christian friends. It is a compromise they feel certain they can make, so long as the Church does not object. Great is their surprise when they discover that long before the Church objects, their friends forsake them. A friend of mine, who came to this country after the Hungarian revolution, told me of his experience in being excluded from Communist society. He held his government post for a while after the Reds came to power. But before long his attendance at Mass began to be mentioned in seemingly casual conversations. It wasn't long before it was made plain to him that no Communist could trust him so long as he attended Mass.

Another friend of mine had a similar experience in an American University. While he was attending college he had a religious experience that brought him into active relationship with the Church. He thought this was purely a personal thing. After all, he had been living a fast and loose life, but he thought his friends were just an average cross section of American life. However, he soon realized his new outlook on life and his tendency to take seriously the Ten Commandments made his friends feel uncomfortable, and they began to avoid him. At first he was disturbed and wondered if he had been over bearing in some way or tried to put on pious airs. Ultimately he had to face the fact that he was just traveling with the wrong crowd, and part of the price of following Christ was the loss of old friends.

Sometimes we pay this price without ever being aware that we have been dropped by old friends, and we have made new ones. But, occasionally, we have to break off a relationship that tears at our very fibre.

We also have to count the cost in time. In our busy world no one has any spare time, and yet God demands of us all a total commitment. Many embark in the Christian faith and then discover that there is a conflict that seemed so small but sometimes looms so large. Weekends used to be carefree, but for some peculiar reason, Christians celebrate Mass on Sunday and so break the continuity of the weekend. We so often depreciate the Catholic whose faith consists of little but a faithful attendance to Sunday Mass, and yet it is not a little thing. A man who believes in God will find time to worship Him. A faithful follower of Christ will want to be in His presence.

God does demand time. Not only on Sunday, but every day. A truly devout person talks with His Lord, not only as a true and intimate friend, but also gives Him time and attention worthy of a king and God.

Finally, God not only wants our hearts and souls, but he also demands something of our material possessions. Non-Church people are often more aware of this than the churched. Often we find people will attend Mass and then begin to inquire about how one goes about coming into the Church. Very often the questioning most pressing on their minds is, "What is it going to cost?" Sometimes they have heard all sorts of horror tales regarding the kind of financial demands the Church makes upon people.

As an old Catholic priest, I tell them, of course, that what they give is between themselves and their God. For some, this is very misleading, for they think they give because the church demands that they give, rather than out of a love of God. Most conscientious inquirers are aware that they will want to bring a gift worthy of someone whom they love and respect. A miserly gift to a king not only seems an affront, but speaks ill of the giver.

And so they count the cost, and usually because it is a privilege rather than an obligation they take it on cheerfully.

But others, who have not been so prudent, find attendance at Mass such a terrible burden that it would be better if they stayed at home. They find it impossible to part company from associations that enable them to turn a dishonest dollar, and so they feel that financially they have taken on a double burden. The very God who demands that they forsake all sinful means of earning a livelihood expects a portion of that which they earn by the honest sweat of their brow.

If life within the Church seems like one great sacrifice of time, of exciting but superficial friends, and too demanding of your purse, perhaps you should pause and reflect upon our text. Lest men mock you for not being able to finish, perhaps you should not proceed to lay a foundation.

But if you have counted the cost, press on, build a foundation upon the rock, that the House of Faith that you will build, will endure forever.

XXVIII

IN TIMES OF SPIRITUAL DRYNESS

INTROIT

Mine eyes are ever toward the Lord: for He shall pluck my feet out of the net.
Turn Thee unto me, and have mercy upon me: for I am desolate and afflicted.
Unto Thee, O Lord, do I lift up my soul: O my God, I trust in Thee: Let me not be ashamed.

In the introit for the Third Sunday in Lent we implore God to help because we are desolate and afflicted.

There is none of us who has not had a period when we felt that we could not pray. These periods of dryness seem to afflict every Christian periodically. No matter how we try, our prayers seem ineffectual and we wonder if God is deserting us. When people come to me and say, "I have prayed and prayed, Father, but it is just as if God doesn't hear."—I can only tell them that these dry spells are natural and have many causes. It is about two of these causes that I wish to speak this evening.

First, I find this often happens when we are so busy with godly things that we do not have time for God. In our living we so often contradict our profession. We hear of pastors who are so busy with the church that they neglect their prayers. Or churches that are so overly organized that they do not have time for people.

I recall reading, one time, about a man who took a safari in Central Africa. It seems that he was in a hurry to reach the interior and drove the native bearers at a terrific pace. Then after the third day, they stopped, and he inquired as to the reason. He was told that the natives were going to wait at that place where they halted until their souls could catch up to their bodies. In our modern fast-moving world, many people must take time for their souls to catch up.

This is the reason why we need to take retreats—or to stop and meditate from time to time. Attendance at Mass was never so important as it is today, for, for many it is the only time they stop—so that their souls might catch up with their bodies.

Whenever we enter a period of dryness we need to stop long enough to examine our activity, to determine whether it is the thing we ought to be doing.

Sometimes we do Godly things in order to shut God out. It is as if we feel by doing these things He could hardly berate us for not listening to His voice. But the question is not "Are we doing good?" but "Are we engaged in the particular activity He would have us do?"

Sometimes we try to do too much. It is such a secure thing, because then no one can scold us for not doing any one thing effectively. We have a ready-made excuse, that there is so much to be done and if only we were relieved of some of our burdens, we could be so much more effective. But God never asks us to do much. He never wants us to be disorganized. If we would stop long enough to heed Him, He would either help us organize our lives or relieve us of some of the burdens that we have taken unto ourselves, without His consent.

It isn't that God won't talk to a disorganized individual. He will, but only long enough to tell us how to get organized so that we might better hear Him and better serve Him.

This period of dryness may only mean that God is waiting for you to lay down your burdens long enough so that He might lighten your load or organize it so that you can carry it more easily.

No one has really caught the meaning of Christianity if he is generous in sharing all that he has with His fellowman, but miserly when it comes to sharing the load. God would have us share not only His gifts to us, but also the burdens He expects us to bear; and the periods of dryness are often His way of telling us that we have kept too much for ourselves.

The second important reason for dry spells is almost the opposite of the first. You may recall that when the children of Israel left Egypt, they stopped by the shores of the Red Sea to pray. Here God told them that it was not the time for prayer but the time to act. Before they could overcome their dry spell they had to act in faith and cross through the sea.

So often I meet people who tell me they are seeking God but they cannot find Him. They attend Mass daily, pray constantly, study the Scriptures, meditate long hours, but a period of dryness has come upon them and God is nowhere to be found.

Keeping in mind the Children of Israel at the Red Sea, I usually begin by asking about their meditation. What one thing can they think of that God has asked them to do? When they tell me what it is, I cannot help but ask another question. "Why should God tell you anything else until you have been obedient to what He has already asked you to do?"

Some of us need to be moving and doing. We need to do the little tasks that God has given us before He can talk to us about bigger tasks.

Occasionally we find men who want to be priests before they have served God as laymen. Any man that comes to me and says he wants to serve the church full time must first tell me what he is doing now—part-time as a layman. Any man or woman who would do great things for God must be faithful to the little tasks.

I remember many years ago a woman telling me about a dry spell she experienced. She had prayed for months that God would grant her request that she go to Africa as a missionary. Not only did He not show her the way, but it seemed to her that He stopped talking to her entirely. One day she realized that God hadn't stopped talking, because day after day, in her meditations, she kept thinking about the pastor's office in her church. There was a lot of work to be done, and the place was in a mess. Finally, it bothered her enough so she went in one day and volunteered her services. In a few days the church office was in good shape, and her dry spell was over. A few weeks later she was offered a job by a large church in the city as a full-time secretary, and she definitely felt that God was calling her to this work. God did have a field of service for her, but He could only show her when she was willing to act.

Often, so often, a dry spell comes because we won't act on something that seems small and trivial. But when God wants us to do something, it is no small thing. The question is not how large is the task, but how great is your obedience?

Every dry spell can be overcome. For some it means to lay our burdens down, for others it means to pick our burdens up. Only God can give us the wisdom to know our own situation.

But God is always more ready to hear than we are to pray. He is always more ready to guide than we are to do his will. He forsakes no man—and no man is ever alone, for He has promised to give to everyone that asketh—not only that which he needs, but in full measure, pressed down and overflowing. May the Lord grant unto you that you desire those things that He would have you have, and that you receive all that you desire.

XXIX
JUDGE NOT

GOSPEL: MATTHEW 7: 1-5

Judge not, that ye be not judged. For with what judgment ye judge, ye shall be judged: and with what measure ye mete, it shall be measured to you again. And why beholdest thou the mote that is in thy brother's eye, but considerest not the beam that is in thine own eye? Or how wilt thou say to thy brother, Let me pull out the mote out of thine eye; and, behold, a beam is in thine own eye? Thou hypocrite, first cast out the beam out of thine own eye; and then shalt thou see clearly to cast out the mote out of thy brother's eye.

This text has much meaning for me, because I have been studying it in relationship to many other related texts.

The Bible presents us with a very important paradox. On page after page we are clearly told that we ARE our brother's keeper. No one can read the Bible without realizing how literally it is meant that we should go into all the world and preach the gospel. Not only preach, but actually, if the occasion calls for it, to correct an errant brother. Further, God holds us responsible for what others do. A modern saint once said that if on the path of life our brother who followed after were to stumble over a stone, we would be held accountable because we removed not the stone from the path.

But with all this concern for our brother we need to keep in mind a basic rule that Jesus gives us. Before we minister to others we must first effectively minister to ourselves. For Jesus saw the the danger that lies in the path of those who would set all the world straight before they themselves became straight.

So often the world is suspicious, and rightly so, of those who preach to them. For many preach not out of concern for their brother, but because preaching has become a means for compensating for their own problems.

One of the most important issues of our day, the fight for civil rights, is confused and beclouded by the number of people who have taken up the cause without properly preparing themselves.

I am struck by the fact that so many of the clergy who have participated in marches down South come from well-to-do white suburban churches in the North. This, to me, is most significant. For without minimizing the needs of the South, or the Negro, if I were to be asked to choose the field where effective missionary preaching is necessary, I would choose the upper-middle-class suburbs.

Here we have a group of citizens who have, in modern parlance, arrived. They have obtained respectable jobs, at prestige salaries, and now have purchased the symbols of success, the 30,000 or

40,000 dollar house in the suburbs. The Church, instead of challenging them, usually caters their favor by offering a bewildering variety of social activity in order to gather them in and so build the church. For these people the message of salvation has no meaning, and they are convinced that they have already found heaven on earth. They are certain that they owe themselves nothing further, unless it is another advancement, or just a little more money.

So few preachers feel capable of challenging this presumptuous conviction that they retreat in frustration, instead of trying to find new means of communicating the Gospel. They emphasize an aspect that they believe is more necessary, or perhaps, easier to see. They would prick the conscience of the suburbanite by telling him that he can't be satisfied to have arrived so long as there are millions who are deprived. And while this is true—it is a distortion. The world is still divided between the haves and the have nots, but along far different lines.

The white middle class suburbs must be counted among the have nots. Why is it we can see so clearly that the country is filled with socially and economically deprived people and fail to feel the same concern for the spiritually deprived?

I sometimes wonder if we who represent the church have not often been guilty of using the world's yardstick as a measure of human need.

Our hearts really do not bleed for those who live in comfortable circumstances and have not found God. We do not see them as poor, or else we do not see the tragedy of poverty in spirit. Have we become so materialistic that we would offer God only to those that have nothing better? If this is not so, why are there no special missionary societies dedicated to taking the gospel to the rich?

We go to the **poor** migrant worker, or the **poor** slum dweller, or the **poor** Negro because we are more concerned with man's material poverty than for his spiritual poverty. But Jesus has rightly seen that if a man would look first to his own spiritual state, he would then see clearly how to remove the mote from his brother's eye. For a man who has tried to cleanse his own soul knows how much more difficult it is to do than to remedy his material lacks.

At the very effort to lift himself out of spiritual poverty he becomes aware of how poor he really is. Only when he himself has sought the spiritual prize can he see clearly how to challenge his brother to do the same.

Without wanting to be critical of anyone who preaches the gospel anywhere, I do wish to stress two needs that I feel are paramount in the church today.

First, we need to learn how to preach the gospel where we are. The people who are closest to us are often the people to whom communication seems closed. Yet, by what devious twisting of the gospel can we ignore the fact that the need is as great here as elsewhere. Think about your friends and associates— they have a desperate need for God in their lives. But you can help them. Jesus suggests a startling but simple way.

By removing from our own lives those things which stand in the way of our spiritual progress, we shall see clearly how to help our neighbor. When we go to our neighbor who has need, we do not seem to judge him when we can say, "This is what I did to solve this problem for myself." In short, Jesus would have us lead the way.

If each man would preach the gospel where he is, and if each man would preach the gospel by beginning with himself—the world would soon come to know **Christ.**

In short, I say to you "Go into the world and preach the gospel to all men, but take heed that first you remove the beam from thine own eye, **for** then thou shalt see clearly to cast the mote out of thy brother's eye.

XXX
ST. STEPHEN

The stoning of St. Stephen has left an indelible impression upon the Christian Church. The death of no other Christian martyr has even remotely had the iufluence as this tragic event, so soon after the death of our Savior Jesus Christ.

It is partially explained by the fact that St. Stephen was the first to die for the faith and partially by the fact that his death set in motion the events that brought about the conversion of St. Paul.

What happened with Paul is something that all of us have in common with him. Paul sought a means to shut God out. God tries to speak to us in so many ways and often through many, many people. But we are seldom in the mood to listen. In many churches, a good and forceful preacher pricks the consciences of the parishoners to the point where they devise ways to get rid of him.

In some Protestant churches they can, and do, change pastors with surprising regularity. In Catholic churches they flood the bishop's offices with their complaints. Even when it doesn't reach this stage, we constantly shut out the preacher by looking, not at our weaknessess, but the preacher's weaknesses.

Jokes about the clergy are often enjoyed more than other types of jokes, because we feel uncomfortable of the challenge they present us Sunday after Sunday from the pulpit. Fortunately, for us who are priests, stoning has gone out of style. But the fact remains that we don't turn God off simply by ridiculing the preacher, banishing him, or in extreme cases, like St. Stephen, stoning him.

God has many voices, and Jesus Himself often chooses to make Himself felt in our lives. Paul, on the road to Damascus, was confronted with Christ, and from Him there was no escape.

Although it is a common human complaint that we everywhere seek God, but he is difficult to find—the fact remains that it is He who is the aggressor.

He has, through His church, provided many voices to speak to you and to me. If we do not heed them—yea, even though we use those despitefully whom He has sent to us—He will never cease trying. The Church has always found new martyrs willing to step in Stephen's shoes, and God has through them and through His own Son Jesus Christ continued to trouble the consciences of men.

As the psalmists once said, though I ascend the highest mountain or descend into the midst of the sea; the Lord is there.

God is ever ready to guide you, direct you, and comfort you. Although He will not force Himself upon you, He will confront you and challenge you constantly. He is an ardent and eager wooer who bids you to accept His love, with all lowliness and meekness. God grant you grace of His Holy Spirit, that you may permit him to enter your heart this day.

XXXI
THE MARTHA SYNDROME

GOSPEL: LUKE 10:38-42

Now it came to pass, as they went, that he entered into a certain village: and a certain woman named Martha received him into her house. And she had a sister called Mary, which also sat at Jesus' feet, and heard his word. But Martha was cumbered about much serving, and came to him, and said, Lord, dost thou not care that my sister hath left me to serve alone? bid her therefore that she help me. And Jesus answered and said unto her, Martha, Martha, thou art careful and troubled about many things: But one thing is needful; and Mary hath chosen that good part, which shall not be taken away from her.

Opposition to the Christian faith takes many forms, but the most common is the Martha syndrome. As Martha went about her daily chores se rationalized her neglect of her honored guest. She convinced herself that what she was doing took precedence over everything else.

Every priest in his daily rounds meets the Marthas of this world. They say, "I don't get to church often, Father, but my religion consists in doing right to others."

One doesn't usually rebuke these people, but instead I make it a practice to commend them on their good beginning. Jesus told us that a concern for others was half of our religious obligation.

But, like Martha, we cannot hide behind our business with strangers, to avoid our service to God. For he has given us life and health, and he provides for our daily needs, and can we not do as much for Him as for some stranger?

How often we tried to avoid one obligation by hiding behind another. In our time we have seen the debate rage between the activists on one hand and the contemplatives on the other. Yet the very Christ who insisted that His disciples leave the Mount of Transfiguration and go down into the market place also drew aside to be alone with His God in the Garden of Gethsemane. Protestants in our day tend to emphasize good works; Catholics prayer and meditation, and Jews the law. But God really wants all of us to be Catholic, Protestant, and Jew, in the sense that he wants us to adhere to His law, serve His people, and to walk in conversation and fellowship with Him.

You cannot pick and choose your obligations to God, but must accept all of them. You cannot be a Protestant to the exclusion of the Catholic emphasis that belongs in your faith. Or as Vatican II discovered, you cannot be a Catholic and avoid certain good works because Protestants performed them. And what Christian can deny his Old Testament roots, for Paul insisted we were all Jews first, if we were to fulfill the gospel of Jesus Christ.

For Martha's sin was not in what she did but in what she neglected. Apparently Mary, at the right time and moment, did her share of the chores; for if she had not, Jesus who was quite conscious of the need to serve, would have rebuked her also. Those of you who serve should not scorn those in contemplation. And those in contemplation should not scorn those in service. Nor will the law by itself suffice. For God demands many things of us, and no man can say he serves Him unless he gives full service.

God would have you be Jew, for the law is to be obeyed by all. He would have you be a Martha, for He insists you do unto your fellowman as you would be done by. He would have you be Mary, for He is the guest in your midst, and He asks that you honor His presence.

At His Table

XXXII
WHAT DO YOU SEE?

When you come to Mass, do you see only Christ? And do you feel that He has eyes for you alone?

Christ did not come into this world only to bring peace to your soul. He came to heal a torn and fragmented world.

At Mass, you may see Christ, but you must also see His disciples. At the Last Supper, Christ was undoubtedly the central figure, but we dare not forget John, Andrew, Peter, yes, and Judas, too.

Day by day we are ripped apart by the greed, the lust, the hate and fears that rule in our hearts. Even as we try to get along and as we struggle to live by rules which we feel will enable us to live peaceably with others, we injure our neighbors and unconsciously open old wounds. Even saints cannot live together without causing one another pain.

Try as we will, we cannot by our own efforts, draw close to one another. Only Christ can bring us together in perfect love and peace.

Here at Mass, when the mind admits a discordant thought, we quickly reject it; for while we are in the presence of Christ, we recognize evil for what it is.

As His servants we leave from here conscious that even as He has loved us and shared His presence with us, so He loves others and shares His presence with whoever will respond to His gracious invitation to sup with Him.

And so we do for Him what we will not do for ourselves. Our love for Christ makes us love all whom He loves.

You've heard, I'm sure, of the G.I. who watched a nun cleaning a leper's sores and remarked, Sister, I wouldn't do that for a million dollars." Her simple reply strikes home, "Neither would I."

Surely for the love of Christ, thousands of religious have gone to minister to the lepers, to the poor and hungry in the most remote areas of the globe, and made sacrifices that without Christ were humanly impossible.

The story of the twelve apostles is amazingly clear of controversy. Even their vying for place in Christ's Kingdom is noteworthy, because it was an exception to the peace that prevailed among them. Where else have you heard of twelve people living together for three years and not one of them breaking out into print to present his side of those controversial years. Even Judas remained to the end; and though he betrayed Christ, he could not live with his betrayal.

It is simply that while we are with Christ, it is difficult to treat others any differently than He would treat them. Therefore, we need to come into His presence frequently, and we need to walk with Him daily; for whenever we get away too far and too long, we lose sight of the fact that He loves others even as He loves us.

So often we establish a casual, rather than an intimate relationship with Christ. The casual Christian knows only that Christ loves him. The Christian who walks with Him constantly and who experiences His presence at Mass regularly knows Christ and shares the love that Christ feels for all mankind.

Christ lives. He is here in the midst of you today. If you will awaken to His presence, you will partake of His love and He will strengthen you by His Spirit so that you may live in peace and like Him love even your enemies.

XXXIII
THIS DO FOR THE RE-PRESENTING OF ME

When I was in Seminary, I was taught that the one new concept that Jesus gave us was the idea of God as Father. Certainly it was new and the fact that it implied that man and God were of the same genus was exciting and filled with hope. Yet the word "Father" means so many different things. When Peter Stuyvesant told the settlers of New Amsterdam that he intended to rule like a Dutch Father, they were appalled, for Dutch Fathers were noted for being harsh and dictatorial.

The 20th Century has given us yet another concept of the word Father, in "The Big Daddy," who gives in to our every wish and desire.

Although Jesus' idea of father included the concept of law giver, and of benefactor, the picture he gives of the Father is far removed from either of these one-sided ideas.

God the Father, as revealed to us by Jesus, is not a remote giver of rules or of gifts, but he deigns to come into the world to minister to our needs.

"Let us see God," the world had cried, and so God sends His own Son, that the world might see and learn through Him, how to live. Even this was not to be a one-time experience. But on the night of the Last Supper, Jesus promised to re-present

Himself whenever the Supper was repeated. Hence, Christians come to worship primarily to be in the presence of Christ.

In this ecumenical age many people are asking, "What is unique about Christianity?" and many dispute the claim that Christianity is in any way unique.

For men all over the world and men of many faiths come together to praise God, to confess their faults, to learn about His laws, and to give thanks. In one sense or another, men and women of all faiths see in God a father who would direct his children and who is concerned with their welfare. And while we who are Christians come to do these things, we come primarily to feel a presence.

We see in God someone who wants to be an intimate part of our lives. Of all the human experiences where we share one another's feelings and thoughts, the most intimate takes place when we sit down together and break bread.

You never really become a part of someone's life until you have a meal together. So many things we do are connected with eating and drinking. Judas is held in such low esteem, not only because he betrayed Jesus, but because after his betrayal his hypocrisy enabled him to break bread with those he had betrayed. Even the crudest man hesitates to speak evil of the man at whose table he has recently sat.

Hence, the fatherhood of God is not some remote figure who handed down the law on Mt. Sinai, or even someone to whom we send our earnest petition, hoping for some good thing.

We have a living father, who through Jesus Christ, dwells among us.

When we seek to find direction for our lives God has provided many helps. We have His Scriptures for our direction, and we have the promise of the guidance of His Holy Spirit. But most important of all, we can go to Him, break bread at His table, and as we recall the events as Christ instituted this great feast, we can experience the joy that comes from His presence.

As we dine with another, although few words might be exchanged, our thoughts and our hearts become united. People who live together, share together and eat together, achieve a oneness of life and purpose. In and through this supper Jesus sought to bring man and God together, so that His prayer in the Garden of Gethsemane might be fulfilled. "That they may all be one; even as Thou, Father, art in me, and I in Thee, that they also may be in us."

XXXIV
CELEBRATION

GOSPEL: LUKE 5:34

And he said unto them, Can ye make the children of the bridechamber fast, while the bridegroom is with them?

Whenever I go into a strange church, I pay very close attention to the faces of those who come forward to receive Holy Communion. For some come with sad countenances, some come weeping, and some, but too few, come with expressions of radiant joy.

Too often and too long we have been told that Christians in our world should be sad. Very often we have been weeping for the sins of the world and mourning for the victims of the world's evil, when we should be rejoicing in the presence of Jesus Christ.

Perhaps we cannot explain the Mass too often. Yet it is a simple direct way of approaching God that the youngest child can comprehend and the mature saint or sinner can appreciate.

First we need to understand that it is a celebration. We come together to celebrate the resurrection of Jesus Christ. We have as our honored guest, the Lord Jesus Christ, whose presence is the reason for our gathering together. With this in mind, how can we come in any other mood but one of great elation and joy? Only one thing may mar our perfect joy, and this is the fact of our own imperfections and our own state of sin. This is why the Mass proper is proceeded by a service of confession.

It seems only natural that before we approach God's holy table that we should confess our shortcomings to Him and seek His forgiveness. And this forgiveness is given to you when you confess your sins, are truly sorry for your offenses, and to resolve to lead a better life in the future.

The Absolution can only be followed by a hymn of thanksgiving, for now the mood must change to one of rejoicing and to one of joyous anticipation.

After we hear the Epistle and Gospel Lesson, we affirm our faith in His coming by reciting together the Apostle's Creed.

The second hymn is truly a Hymn of preparation. We have offered our prayers, both for specific individuals for whom we have special concern and for those who do not share with us this joyous experience. Then as the priest prepares the altar, we offer one last prayer for our most urgent concerns.

The beginning of the Mass takes us back through the centuries to an Upper Room in the city of Jerusalem where Jesus celebrated His Last Supper with His diciples.

It is both a reminder that He has commanded us to meet together in His Name to celebrate this feast and a reminder of His promise to us—promise that He would be present, that He would be in our midst whenever we gathered together in His Name.

Accenting this, and in grateful anticipation, we offer our prayers, and we lift up our hearts in words of praise and thanksgiving.

Finally, the moment that we have awaited has come. The priest offers the prayer to the Holy Spirit and we prepare ourselves to receive our Lord and Savior Jesus Christ. We receive the symbols of bread and wine with our lips, but we receive the Body and Blood of our Lord Jesus Christ with our hearts.

We come to feel a presence and to take home with us a renewed spirit and mind wholly dedicated to live with Him, with whom we have spent these few moments together, eating and drinking and singing psalms and making melody.

Rejoice in the Lord always, and again I say Rejoice, for the Lord has come into your midst and you have received Him in your hearts.

Before His Throne

XXXV
TO DO GOOD FOR THE LORD'S SAKE

Never in the history of the Church have so many people been intent on doing so much good. This should truly be cause for rejoicing, and if it were all for God's glory we would sing "hosannas."

But it is so easy to busy ourselves doing many things that merely seem virtuous and good. It is equally easy to do these things for the wrong reasons. The praise heaped upon donors and the publicity given their good works has cast a shadow upon the good works of many.

Yet most of us, if we were honest with ourselves, would have to admit that much of the good receive some reward for our acts. At the very least, we expect that God will be grateful; and if He will not reward us for our acts, He will at least spare us any undue hardships and suffering.

For many of us, suffering comes as a shock and a disappointment, and we ask, "Why should this happen to me after all the good things I have done?"

Do we really believe that man should be rewarded for doing good? Surely, if it is our greatest pleasure to do good things for God and man, the PLEASURE is reward enough.

Jeremy Taylor advised us, "In every action reflect upon the end, and in your undertaking it, consider why you do it, and what you propound to yourself for a reward, and to your action and its end."

Modern Christians are in need of less exhortation to do good and more exhortation to love God. To urge man to do good only leads to a self-conscious form of good works that feeds men's vanity.

On the other hand, to learn to truly love God moves a man to do good works for God's sake, and because God loves man.

We need to lose sight of ourselves and our actions and see God only.

In fact, in so many instances we see Christian people so busy doing good that they do not have time for God. We see mothers devoted to community service, from Cub Scouts to P.T.A., who do not have sufficient time for their families.

I have heard laymen plead they had no time for the work of the Church because they had so many meetings of service or fraternal organizations. I have known clergymen whose devotional life was meager because they were so busy doing the Lord's work.

We love his work, but all too often we do not love Him.

To do good, yes, but let us do it for the love of God and let it pour out naturally and easily from our fellowship with Him. If we seek Him first, all the rest shall be added unto us.

XXXVI
WHO ARE YOU?

GOSPEL: MATTHEW 6:33

But seek ye first the kingdom of God, and his righteousness; and all these things shall be added unto you.

I have on many occasions preached on the New Morality, and, I suspect my hearers must have said to themselves, "Isn't there anything at all that he likes about the New Morality?"

If by that term we mean those things currently receiving emphasis, I am happy to say that there is.

When the new generation says "We want to be free to be ourselves," they are repeating the age old cry of the saints.

In our time it was Thomas Merton who was its most ardent apostle. But Merton was a well-honed thinker who raised the critical question of "How do I discover my true self?" For he points out that man is not like a tree or an animal whose selves are predetermined by God. Man is left free to be whatever he would like. You can deny your true self, if you wish. Hence, says Merton, "God alone possesses the secret of my identity. He alone can make me who I am, or rather, He alone can make me who I will be when I at last fully begin to be."

Unfortunately, the many who say, "We want to be ourselves," are content to live life at animal level. But we miss the truth about man if we see him only as an animal. For man is made in the image of God. Not to accept this and strive to achieve it is to refuse the fullness of existence.

This is why sin is a reality which we cannot ignore. For sin stands between man and his real self. When we offend God we cut ourselves off from the only one who reveals to us what we can become.

When we come to Mass we seek "to identify ourselves with Him in Whom is hidden the reason and fulfillment of our existence."

Too many are crying, "Who am I?" The answer is not to be found on the psychiatrist's couch, nor by inward searching and contemplation.

Ask the question, my friends, of your Creator. He who has made you is anxious that you fulfill the purpose of your creation and achieve the full stature He intended for you.

The way for self discovery is to discover God. In discovering Him, I will find myself and if my true self I will find Him.

For the truth of Christ prevails that if we seek The Kingdom of God and His righteousness, all the rest will be added unto us.

XXXVII
HERE AM I

I KINGS 3:4

And the king went to Gibeon to sacrifice there; for that was the great high place; a thousand burnt offerings did Solomon offer upon that altar. And the Lord called Samuel, and he answered: "Here am I."

Much of what we call prayer is very ineffective, because it begins within ourselves. The best prayer is our response to God's call. It begins with God, who is forever trying to communicate with us. Many in the world lack this awareness of God. They are not tuned into God, and their ears are filled with the sounds of our noisy, noisy world.

Oswald Chambers says we will never truly learn from God until He gets us alone. In the New Testament we read constantly that the greatest learning experiences of the disciples took place when they were alone with Jesus.

God seldom shouts at us while we are in the midst of the crowd, or at some great distance. When He does, it is only to draw us out from among the crowd so that He might hold an intimate con-conversation with us.

God wanted to talk with Samuel, and He called him while he slept. The fact that Samuel was responding to God's call made all the difference in the world. So many Christians are so intent upon calling God, or so intent on what they have to say to God, that they never hear Him. In any event they do not respond to God.

Perhaps this is why prayer has ceased to have appeal. Too many of us conceive of it as something initiated by us, and all we need to do is wait for God to respond. Hence, we ask God for favors, and while we are voicing these, we are missing opportunities. For God is constantly whispering suggestions to us. He is directing us to this opportunity or that opening, and we do not hear.

So intent are we with our vain trifles, we miss the Master's voice that is directing us to His Kingdom and all the gifts that await us within.

Truly the Psalmist spoke wisely when he directed us to "Be still and know God."

If you would pray, first open your hearts and minds in meditation. Unless you do this, you dishonor God. For when a man comes into the presence of one who is greater than he, he first waits, and when he is spoken to, he gives answer.

When you can respond to God's call, "Here I am, O Lord," your life in Christ will begin in earnest.

XXXVIII

FILLED WITH THE SPIRIT

EPISTLE: EPHESIANS 5:15-21

See then that ye walk circumspectly, not as fools, but as wise, Redeeming the time, because the days are evil. Wherefore be ye not unwise, but understanding what the will of the Lord is. And be not drunk with wine, wherein is excess; but be filled with the Spirit; Speaking to yourselves in psalms and hymns and spiritual songs, singing and making melody in your heart to the Lord; giving thanks always for all things unto God and the Father in the name of our Lord Jesus Christ. Submitting yourselves one to another in the fear of God.

Be filled with the Spirit. We hear so many sermons about the cross that we sometimes forget the unique joy that comes to those who are Christian.

While it is true that we are the burden bearers of the world, it is equally true that we are a chosen people who have received some very special blessings.

I could speak of many joys that only Christians experience, but I want to talk with you this evening about three which seem to me to be particularly significant.

First, in a day when so many find life to be meaningless, the Christian has a sense of purpose. It is something we take for granted, but it is a very wonderful thing. Today we see thousands upon thousands wandering over the face of the earth endlessly looking for meaning. Some have concluded there is no meaning to life and that they might just as well pass the time smoking pot and living in idleness. The tragedy of so many lives without purpose is that they engage in a never ending pursuit of purchasing things, hoping that some one thing is going to satisfy. Only when life is almost over do they realize that nothing can satisfy, for each man must feel he is significant or he feels no peace. Only when I know that God has created me for a purpose can I feel that my creation has meaning. For what could I own that would be one half so satisfying as the knowledge that God looked at the vast universe and concluded that I was needed, and therefore He gave me life and a mission to accomplish for Him.

A second joy, unique to Christians, comes from the knowledge that no mistake on our part can destroy life's meaning for me. If I sin and disobey Him, He is ever ready to forgive and take me back into His fold and assign new tasks for me to do. If I spoil His plans for me, He has a new plan and a new use for my life. Because God is patient and kind, He will stand by me when I am weak, love me even when I am faithless, wait for me even though I am long away from Him.

God is ever ready to give me a fresh start in life, and as long as I breathe I know He has not given up on me. I am never too poor of talent, too old or too late. Now is the accepted time of salvation, and life can always be meaningful to the man or woman who will accept God at His word, that He beckons sinners to repent and come into His Service.

Finally, I am not expected to overcome the world by my strength alone.

How often we hear at the end of a tragic life the words, "Poor dear, she had no one to turn to." A Christian is never without someone to turn to. God is ever ready to comfort us in our sorrows, to strengthen us in our temptations and to guide us through the difficult paths.

In 1929 the stock market crash was the end of the road for many that did know God. Money had been their god, and when they lost it, they lost also their friends and resorted to jumping out of windows.

But no Christian need ever be friendless. No Christian is ever alone. But one of the great joys of our faith is being able to step into the darkness and there take hold of the hand of God and walk into the future with confidence.

The burdens of our faith are not to be compared with the joys that come to those who believe. No wonder we can be filled with the spirit, singing and making melody to the Lord.

XXXIX
TODAY BE IN PARADISE WITH HIM

LUKE 23:43

"And Jesus said unto him, Verily I say unto thee, today shalt thou be with me in paradise."

Why, with all the people around, does Jesus offer the gift of paradise to a thief?

In the three years of his ministry, Jesus never once promised paradise immediately to anyone, but to this thief that hung upon the cross.

Our first difficulty in understanding it lies in our view of the man's sin. None of us are thieves, and hence we consider our own condition to be somewhat more favoroble than this man's.

But sin, all sin, is nothing more or less than estrangement from God. The man who steals may be no further from God than the successful businessman, or tradesman, who has no time for God. What difference does the reason make? What matters is whether we love God or whether we don't But we too often hide ourselves in our cloak of respectability; and since we don't cause God any trouble, we feel He should be satisfied with us.

Christ could offer paradise to a repentant thief just as easily as He could offer it to you and me when we humble ourselves enough to come to Him.

If comparisons were in order, and I suspect they are not, we don't really know very much about the thief. It may be that He compares favorably with us. One could be crucified as a thief by the Romans for very small crimes. Then too, He might have been a basically good man who had a temporary lapse.

I am inclined towards this because of the very unusual events of this day. Consider for a moment this man's situation. He is condemned to die upon a cross. It was a common way to die in those days, but this man does not die in an ordinary way. In the midst of his suffering he considers someone else besides himself, and he recognizes the divine nature of Christ.

There are few of us who can raise above our own suffering and our own troubles to consider others. There are few today who can recognize God when they see Him in their midst. This thief, as he was called, was able to do both.

This insight into Jesus did not come about instantaneously. A man is not ignorant of God one minute and knowledgeable the next. Behind this recognition there had to be years of searching and years of fellowship with God.

What happened on Golgotha was a mutual recognition. The thief recognized Christ even as Christ recognized the godly qualities of the thief. the thief.

Christ hangs upon the Cross today, crucified by the ignorance and the evil of our world. You and I feel burdened with our own cross of troubles—can we, like the thief, rise above our troubles, and do we, like the thief, see God in our midst? For when we can see God in our midst and we can rise above our cross of trouble to see the need of others, then can Christ say to us,

"Today shalt thou be with Me in paradise."

XL
ENTHUSIASM

> The Spirit of the Lord filleth the world; Hallelujah. Let the righteous be glad: let them rejoice before God: yea, let them exceedingly rejoice. Hallelujah, Hallelujah.

Many people seem to forget that the introit for Pentecost Sunday strikes a note of enthusiasm. Unfortunately since the first Pentecost, many Catholics seem to take the attitude that enthusiasm is something better left to the sects. Years ago at the church in Deering, N.H., a neighbor to the church came over to complain about the ringing of the church bell at the hour of 8:30 a.m. I must confess that his attitude is closer to the thinking of the majority of Christian people than mine. His attitude is that religion is all right, but there is a time and place for everything, and church bells should be mute at a time when good people want to sleep.

But if he viewed the resurrection and Pentecost as I do, he wouldn't want to sleep. This is the time to wake, and it is about time we Christians did something to wake up the world. How can anyone sleep on a day set aside to commemorate the resurrection of Jesus Christ?

Even though we have been celebrating the event for 2,000 years, we can never really become blasé about it.

On Sunday morning we should be up with the sun and the ringing of the bells and the firing of cannon should announce the day to a sleepy and sleeping nation.

One reason why the gospel has not caught fire may be that we are too casual about it.

I am well aware that the blatant and sometimes noisy sectarian is offensive to some people—but actually his enthusiasm may not be at fault.

What disturbs some people is an unreasonable enthusiasm, but I think we have logical and sound reasons for sounding excited. But even more important, those that offended are not offended by the enthusiasm, but by the challenge given to their own complacency and indifference.

Christ has come into the world, and every last excuse for not coming to God has been stripped from us.

Mankind must wait no more, for both John and Jesus have announced that the day of salvation is at hand. We are told to rejoice and to sing praises to God. If the language sounds strange to our ears it is because we are not attuned to the Christian gospel.

It is primarily a message of joy, and the eccitement that characterizes the gospel grows out of the thrilling and tremendous events of Easter Day.

In the language of our day, if you want to be your reserved calm, self during the week, alright, but on Sunday,—at Mass—live a little—join in the Mass with enthusiasm and give praise to Him with psalms and with singing.

XLI
REJOICE!

GOSPEL: MATTHEW: 5:12

"Rejoice, and be exceedingly glad; for great is your reward in heaven; for so persecuted they the prophets which were before you."

It is amazing to me that among the manifold changes and so-called reforms in the church, no one has suggested that we drop the observance of All Saints Day.

While it is true that millions reared in parochial schools have strong memories concerning the heroics of their favorite saint, by and large the saint has ceased to be a hero among a large part of our society.

I cannot remember the number of times someone has made the remark to me, "Well, I'm not trying to be a saint." In almost every case the remark was superfluous, but why aren't we trying to be saints? For a saint is someone who has found God, and is this not the purpose of our existence? One might say that the saint is someone who has been successful in this life!

Our 20th Century world puts so much stress on success—it is a shame that it seeks after success in those things which are trivial and finite. At least in the past five decades, although the majority did not seek after sainthood, a vast host of men and women in the religious orders made this their professed goal. Most Catholics knew of at least one nun or brother who seemed to be striving after sainthood. The boy in parochial school who got his knuckles rapped with a ruler by some irate sister may have wondered how anyone with such a disposition could aspire to sainthood, but he never doubted but what this was her goal. He was sure She wasn't going to make it, but he respected her for trying.

I, for one, would regret it very much if the cloistered brothers and nuns were to disappear from our world. We need someone to give witness to the ultimate goal of life. I am not saying that the way to find God is via the cloister, for this may not be the best way. But the cloister has been our most visible witness to the Christian conviction that we are here to serve God. You see too many in our day and age who do not understand this. They sometimes say we are here to serve others. This isn't exactly true. In God's eyes your neighbor is worth no more or no less than you. Service to your neighbor has worth only when it is the will of God.

We too often fail to realize that giving to others is a mixed blessing. The mother who sacrifices herself for a son or daughter has often unwittingly sacrificed the son or daughter as well.

The only daughter who has sacrificed her own happiness to care for a lonely mother has often created a heartless creature who has spoiled the happiness of everyone around her, including her own.

It is God who gives, and it is God who takes away. The saint is someone who has learned to be in tune with God's wishes and to give as He directs. The saint lives not for others but for God, and through Him he serves others in the only way that brings an unmixed blessing.

It is said, that this generation wants to serve mankind. If this is true, then this generation needs to learn from the saints how mankind can best be served.

The Sermon on the Mount should not be misread. For Jesus has issued a call to all to give of themselves, but it is a qualified call. He asks that you be meek, that you hunger for justice, that you practice mercy, and that you seek after peace. But note this, though you do all this and endure the persecution that follows, you do it not for mankind but for His sake. Only in this way will mankind be blessed and only in this way will you find your recompense. Then may you, "Rejoice and exult, because your reward is great in heaven."

XLII

PRAISE YE THE LORD!

PSALM 96:4a

For the Lord is great, and greatly to be praised; he is to be feared above all gods.

The writers of the Psalms by no means proclaimed all of the gospel, but they did lay the one foundation from which we can surely find God.

Of the greatness of God, they felt no doubt, and of the certainty that He should be praised they had no question.

What is lacking in the world today is not mere belief in God, not just a mere acceptance of his existence, but a profound, deep and abiding conviction concerning His great glory.

Until we can look at His handiwork and feel awe, we have not seen Him. Until we see His face in the innocent face of children and in the fragile faces of the pansies, we are insensitive to His Presence. I'm not speaking of the sentimental love of natural beauty or a vague kind of feeling that God is all around us. The psalmist was moved in a way that we lack. "Sing unto the Lord a new song: sing unto the Lord, all the earth."

He looked upon the same mountains, the same sky, the same flowers, and he moved heavenward. He did not content himself with saying, "I see

God everywhere," but he said, "I see God everywhere and therefore will I sing praises unto His name, and serve Him with Thanksgiving." So real was the God he saw in the world about him that he was stirred to action. Since it was God, and not nature he worshipped, he sought out God's will and did it.

The world has not changed very much, in spite of thousands of years of abuse. God's world still shows through the chaos and haze wrought by man.

For it to have meaning for us, we must do as the psalmist say.

First, become truly excited and moved by what we see.

Second, resolve to give glory to God by giving service to Him and to mankind.

And finally, to give witness to the heathen, that the Lord reigneth and that He shall judge the people righteously.